MY EXPERIMENTS WITH ~~TRUTH~~ ORGANISATIONAL RESILIENCE:

Part II

'My Experiments with Truth' is Mahatma Gandhi's book, so I didn't want to use that title.

DAMAN DEV SOOD, FBCI, FBCS, CBCI
Director – DBD Training & Consultancy (OPC) Private Limited
IEEE Ambassador
Past Chair – IEEE Computer Society Delhi Section Chapter
Member Champion – IEEE India MOVE, Partner Relations Committee
IEEE Computer Society Distinguished Contributor, (Inaugural Class)

Chair – Public Relations & Publication Standing Committee,
IEEE Delhi Section

BCI's C&R Business Continuity Manager of the Year Award India 2009
BCI's Merit Award Global 2012
BCI's Continuity & Resilience Contributor Award Middle East 2020
(and Global Finalist)
DRII's Lifetime Achievement Award 2021(Finalist)
BCI's Continuity & Resilience Contributor Award Global, India & South Asia 2021
BCI's Hall of Fame
ILA's Global Outstanding Leadership Award 2021
DRII's Lifetime Achievement Award 2021(Finalist)
DRII's Lifetime Achievement Award 2022(Finalist)
Qualified Independent Director
(Ministry of Corporate Affairs, Govt. of India scheme)
Certified International Trainer, Certified Corporate Trainer

International Trainer & Consultant|| 14000+ hours Training/ Teaching|| Speaker|| Author|| Researcher|| Auditor|| Assessor|| ISO 22301/ NCEMA 7000|| ISO 31000|| BS 11200|| ISO 22316||
Organisational Resilience|| BCM|| Crisis Management|| Enterprise Risk Management|| Operational Risk Management|| Operational Resilience|| Cybersecurity|| Mentor|| LinkedIn Invited Contributor|| LinkedIn Training and Development (HR) Top Voice||
Qualified Independent Director

Dedicated to Global Resilience (personal, professional Business, IT, Finance, Operational, Organisational, IT,…..). And to my family (My Organisational Resilience journey would not be complete and successful without their support). Special thanks to my wife Bhavna who has always been a great support. I owe thanks to Anchita Sood and Tanuj Sood for editing the book and designing the covers respectively. And the Organisational Resilience experiments would not be complete without my clients and associates worldwide, so they deserve thanks from me. Many stories in the book have been initiated based on some paper/ article by HBR, McKinsey, KPMG etc. so they deserve a special mention.

A Note to Readers

Foreword

Christine F Miller

An international emergency and business continuity consultant and Another resilience champion based in Australia

Daman Sood is such a generous and sharing colleague and friend to many globally. This latest edition, Part II of his experiments in organizational resilience continues to expand our understanding of how to strengthen resilience in ourselves, our businesses/organizations, our communities, and our countries.

More than 4 years ago, Daman started working on Organizational Resilience. In the opening remarks to his Part I book on his organizational resilience experiments, Daman reflected on these phrases (p 9), which continue to hold true for his Part II book.

A risk managing, learning, and continually improving organization is a Resilient Organization. And Resilient People make Resilient Organizations.

Part II focuses initially on personal resilience, then moves onto the challenges of business or organizational resilience, including

comparative cases studies between the Bank of England and the Central Bank of Ireland. Daman's book concludes with how personal resilience leads to operational resilience and achieving organizational resilience. Throughout this journey, the reader benefits from many insights and tips that we all take to heart and implement to strengthen resilience. The challenges of an increasingly unreliable planet will require all of us to dig deep and become more resilient in all aspects of our lives.

Dr. David Rubens, Executive Director, The Institute of Strategic Risk Management speakers about resilience being fast thinking agreed in the response phase. What Daman offers is a slower and more considered approach to resilience. There is room for both approaches as we broaden our understanding of resilience and how to do better.

It is my pleasure to continue to support Daman's continuing work on personal and organizational resilience. I commend this book to you and encourage you to read and learn.

Contents

I begin with these phrases that I have invented since I started working on Organisational Resilience about 4 years ago:

A risk managing, learning, and continually improving Organisation is a Resilient Organisation.

And

Resilient People make Resilient Organisations.

So, it's clear that my approach and this book will talk a lot about people.

What this book contains is not what I have done in the Organisational Resilience space, but what I believe Organisational Resilience is and can do. There will be less of what is so obvious (e.g. Business Continuity Management, Crisis Management, Risk Management, IT Disaster Recovery, Information/ Cyber Security etc.) and lot more of the not so obvious portions of the Organisational Resilience e.g. People, Board, Relationships, Creativity, Innovation, Empowerment, Procurement, Finance, Strategy etc.

Part I was published earlier this year. There may be some references back to that book. Chapter Numbers and Infographic Numbers have been kept in continuation from Part I.

Part I had snippets, this one Part II has some longer chapters, some focusing on Organisational Resilience in a particular sector e.g. Healthcare.

This book contains three guest chapters from fellow professionals (who also happen to be my past students) with the sole objective of encouraging more fellows to write their views and experiences. They remain responsible for the content and quality of the portion that they have contributed. I am happy that I have been able to inspire at least three fellow professionals to embark on the journey of being published authors. I wish them all the best!

The fourth guest chapter is from a seasoned professional/ author.

6 Learn Car Racing and Be Resilient!

McKinsey partners define current state (coming out of Covid-19 Pandemic) as in a turn on the racing track.[1]

As in racing, you make the big moves on the turns, not the straights. Coming out of COVID-19, we're in a turn, so now's the time to make changes in resilience, strategy, and operations.

This is the time when there is a possibility of slowing down happens after each success and the world has managed Covid-19 Pandemic successfully. The increased risk is that the world is getting tired also having managed the longest crisis of the history, possibly. This is the turn that the McKinsey partners are referring to and are raising caution to make big moves.

They go further in saying "In the longer term, businesses will learn that resilience is a capability they need to master, not an alarm button they hit after the fire has started. It's been neglected because it was traditionally seen as an expensive muscle to have. Now Organisations are realizing it's an expensive muscle not to have. And modern technology makes it possible to build resilience efficiently—the only way to do it in today's world."

So, its action time have you recorded the lessons learnt from Covid-19 Pandemic Management? I have not yet been able to

---

[1]Arvind Govindarajan and Marco Vettori, *"What does resilience mean in capital and balance-sheet management?"* Mckinsey & Company- Commentary, July 30, 2021 available at- *https://www.mckinsey.com/business-functions/risk-and-resilience/our-insights/what-does-resilience-mean-in-capital-and-balance-sheet-management*

see a comprehensive document from an Organisation showing what happened, how (and how much) we were impacted, what did we do, what went well, what could be done differently, and the lessons learnt. Specifically, did you record the financial impact (how much did you lose) and human impact (how many were sick to what degree and how many lost lives to Covid-19). How much did you spend on managing Covid-19 Pandemic some heads that I recommend are:

1. IT expenditure (mostly providing desktops/ laptops, connectivity).
2. Other infrastructure expenditure (desks and chairs).
3. Additional allowances, if any.
4. Support to the families of those who lost their lives.
5. Vaccination:

a. Staff
b. Staff's families
c. Contractors
d. Contractors' families

And the biggest question to be asked, to be able to call ourselves truly resilient Organisation that we survived Covid-19 Pandemic is not enough, will we be able to spend such amounts again if required? Have we made such provisions in the budget now? If not, then resilience is far away.

7 Innovation and Organisational Resilience

BELIEVE IT OR NOT!

NBA has a CIO (Chief Innovation Officer)!

Then all other Organisations need it for sure.

1. Growth and change across all dimensions need to be the mindset of every person in the Organisation.
2. Think every day: How can I challenge the status quo and do something differently?
3. The key is: take a great idea, share it quickly, and implement it across the Organisation.
4. You have a bow and arrows and a quiver, and you need to pull the right arrow out of the quiver at the right time.

(4 points as excerpts from Amy Brooks, Chief Innovation Officer, NBA discussions with McKinsey).[2]

[2] Eric Roth, *"The Committed Innovator: A conversation with Amy Brooks of the NBA"*, Mckinsey & Company-Podcast, June 20, 2021 available at- *https://www.mckinsey.com/business-functions/strategy-and-corporate-finance/our-insights/the-committed-innovator-a-conversation-with-amy-brooks-of-the-nba*

Picture34: Innovation in Organisational Resilience

I talk of innovation and how it can lead to new heights in overall performance of the Organisation in my 3 days Organisational Resilience Specialist course.

The infographic on Oicture34 above shows some powerful words that I make use of while defining and explaining Organisational Resilience and its benefits. Organisational Resilience is the vaccine to put new life in your company.

8 Old Habits Die Hard!

What does it take to build scalable new businesses inside of an older, more established company?[3]

We knew that the new/ green trees bend, old trees break (or are cut down) they don't have flexibility.

This is the fact about human body also the young ones generally have more flexible bones.

And this is true about companies also long/ well established companies have in-built resistance to change. Oh, here I go about Organisational Resilience. Yes, the old/ well established Organisations need it more than anyone else!

I have found that inefficiencies creep in over a period, so a thorough look is needed in the companies that have well/ long established BCMS even if certified for decades. (BCM is a portion in Organisational Resilience). They are, I say, in Maintenance Mode. They know how to maintain their BIA, BC Plans etc. Ask them to conduct afresh or ask them how they conducted they won't be able to tell. They may not even be able to find the original process and template.

It's very important for any company contemplating agile to create a very compelling "why." says Bart.

---

[3] Bart Schlatmann, CEO Allianz Direct, *"A digital-business builder: An interview with the CEO of Allianz Direct"*, Mckinsey & Company, June 25, 2021 available at- https://www.mckinsey.com/business-functions/mckinsey-digital/our-insights/a-digital-business-builder-an-interview-with-the-ceo-of-allianz-direct

I establish this BIG WHY for Organisational resilience in my Organisational Resilience Specialist course.

You may like to pick up a task to make notes about which chapters talk about the Big Why of Organisational Resilience.

Elsewhere in the book, I have written about my copyrighted concept 'Resilience OPD' which again is recommended for old/ well established companies

9 How to Be a Big Boss!

The term generally is taken to be negative e.g. acting like a big boss or you are not the big boss! In my earlier book 'My Experiments with BCM' I have devoted a chapter to this as 'I am the boss; I know the business'! The CEO of that bank insulted (my view) his team in front of a third party (me) and didn't display the characteristics of leading a resilient Organisation.

How you get along with your manager can shape your health, happiness, and productivity.[4]

She calls it the 'Boss Factor':

- bosses have an enormous influence on workers' well-being
- people's job satisfaction has an enormous influence on their overall life satisfaction
- things like health and mental health are obviously important for whether somebody's happy in their lives
- then comes whether they're happy in their job
- and for that their relationship with their boss matters the most
- bosses have a huge influence on financial performance of businesses and also on the well-being of the workers, and hence, the business's societal impact

The above can easily be transformed into Organisational Resilience Cycle:

[4] Terra Allas, "*The boss factor*" , Mckinsey & Company, June 25, 2021 available at- *The boss factor | McKinsey*

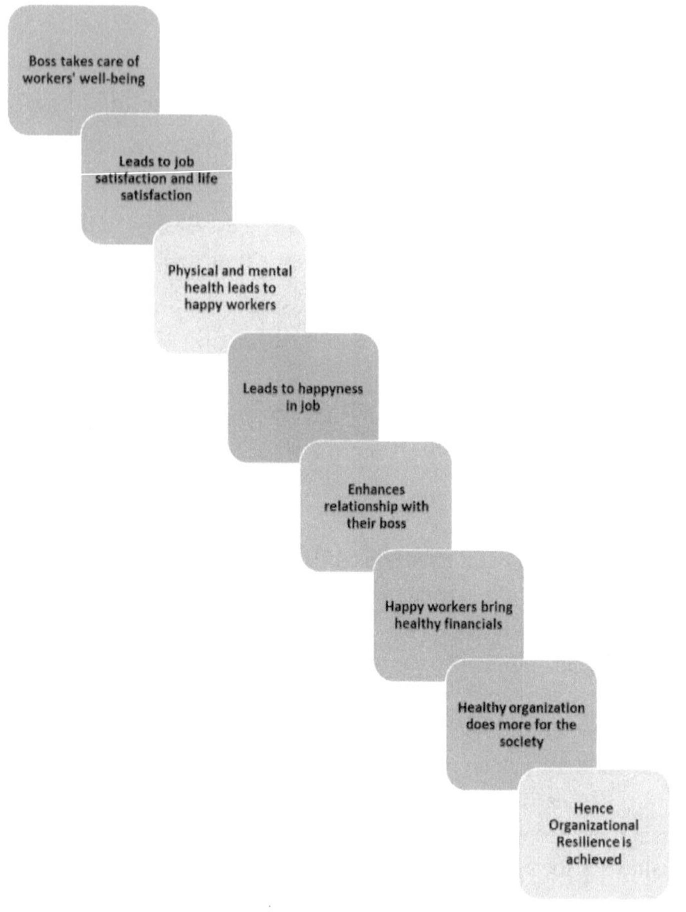

Picture35: Organisational Resilience Steps

BUT SHOULD IT BE ONE WAY? Or the subordinates also play some role?

I touch upon building, maintaining, and enhancing (nurturing) RELATIONSHIPS with all relevant interested parties in my Organisational Resilience Specialist Course. The cycle above shows the impact of relationship between just two entities or interested parties when all interested parties are taken care of, the benefits will be manifolds. Yes, there are too many relationships to be built and maintained, hence resilient organisations are not built in a day (like Rome was not built in a day!) t's a journey of transformation.

10 Relationships

These relationships are equal to their Interested Parties, hence one of the first steps in Organisational Resilience journey is to identify all relevant interested parties for yourself. And their needs and expectations from you. Not an easy job!

These interested parties include (not definitive list) employees, employees' families, shareholders, customers, vendors, regulators, competitors, special interest groups, trade bodies etc.

Picture36: Organisational Resilience Components-3

A happy employee is a good resource to be a Resilient Organisation. Here are some keys to keep the employees happy i.e. building trust in this relationship:

- Money is the greatest motivator - (I ran a LinkedIn poll around this, and there were a good number of disagreements so we can change it to 'money is one of the greatest motivators')
- Employee satisfaction rate
- Employee engagement activities - (One of the activities some Organisations run is Annual Family Day Smartly extending the trust to another relationship i.e. families)
- Employee appraisal process
- Delivering on the commitment to employees
- Walking the talk by the top management
- 'Employer of choice' target
- Personal development process
- Training program (Some Organisations mandate a certain number of training days per year for all employees)
- General 'caring' attitude/culture
- Employee suggestion scheme
- General 'listening' attitude/culture
- Whistle-blower process

11 Resilience OPD

A human body undergoes changes, sometimes (mostly) not visible with naked eyes. The same happens with the Organisations, but worryingly much faster.

People are advised to undergo a regular health check-up after the age of 40 or so to detect any changes and the doctor then prescribes in advance this is personal resilience.

A step forward in Organisational Resilience is my concept of Resilience OPD.

The consultants (having experience in OB-HR, BCM, Risk Management, Crisis Management, GRC, ITDR, Organisational Resilience, Legal etc. at least one from each of these fields) will be available. The patients (Organisations) can come with existing reports (plans as they may have, any other assessments done internally/externally). The Organisational Resilience Consultants will have the first look/ discussions and will recommend them to go to the most appropriate consultant in other categories, who will have further discussions and will recommend some immediate corrections and additional diagnosis that may take time and will produce additional reports for them to prescribe further improvements.

My Organisational Resilience Assessment Tool (copyrighted) can be used in this diagnosis and will help to draw up the roadmap to corrections or improvements. No need to do a lot at the same time, based on the Red, Amber, Green indicators, the tool will help to find out areas needing focus, the Organisation then can additionally think of other parameters (like Organisational priorities, strategic plans etc.) to set the priorities for corrective activities.

This tool provides a modular/pick-and-choose (any of the 20 boxes that I talk about) approach. No need to go big bang that will have huge pressure on resources and heartbreaks may tend to have 'give up' or 'it never works' tendency. Another benefit of the modular approach is to run a small project (on one or two boxes) in 'pilot' mode learn, improve, and then expand the scope.

Special targets will be the Organisations that have had these programs (Risk, Crisis, BC, ITDR etc.) running for a long period (up to-10 years). It is expected that like the human body, some changes might have occurred which may not be so obviously visible. This OPD will help bring those inefficiencies out to help Organisations to draw up improvement plans.

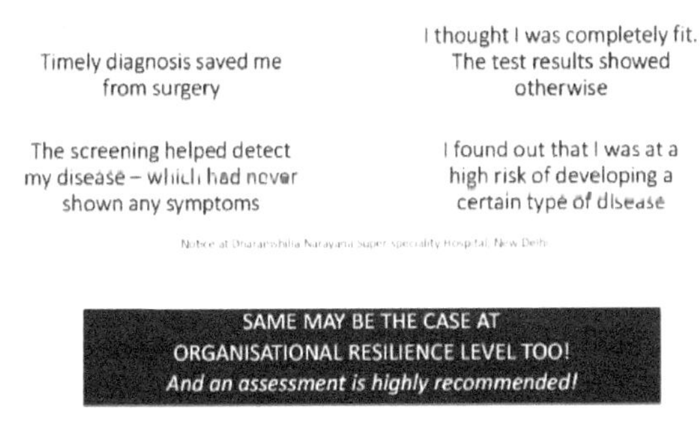

Picture37: Sample Notice at A Hospital

I also recommend that this deep cleansing service through Resilience OPD is repeated after every five years as I expect this to be a reasonable period for inefficiencies to have crept in any Organisation due to multiple changes internal/external context, lethargy, movement of people out of the department/Organisation.

Organisational Resilience is a journey of transformation. No Organisation can ever be 100% resilient, so a continued focus and effort is required.

According to an HBR study, the failure rate of transformation programs is around 70%!

This study provides three simple tips to ensure successful company transformation programs, as:

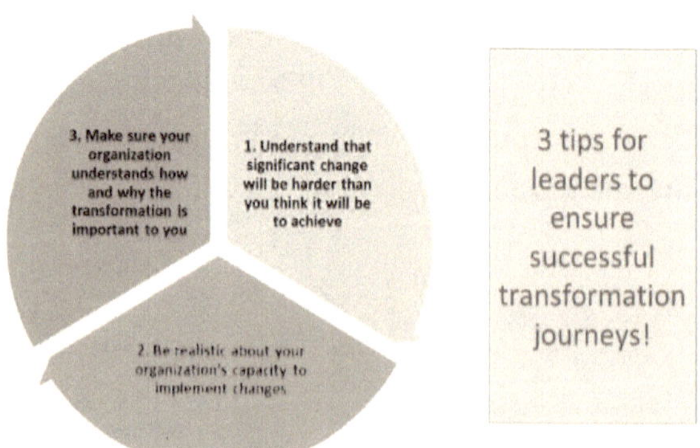

Picture38: Tips for successful transformations

Full details available at How Leaders Get in the Way of Organizational Change[5]

---

[5] Ron Carucci, *"How Leaders Get in the Way of Organizational Change"* Harward Business Revew, April 30, 2021 available at- *https://hbr.org/2021/04/how-leaders-get-in-the-way-of-*

Do your employees understand the 'purpose' of your existence? (look in the Organisational Resilience Snippets in Part I of the book).

Organisational-change?utm_medium=email&utm_source=newsletter_daily&utm_campaign=dailyalert_notactsubs&deliveryName=DM130585 .

12 The First Step Identify Your Interested Parties

The infographic shows Interested Parties as defined in ISO 22313 and Stakeholders as defined by McKinsey & Company.

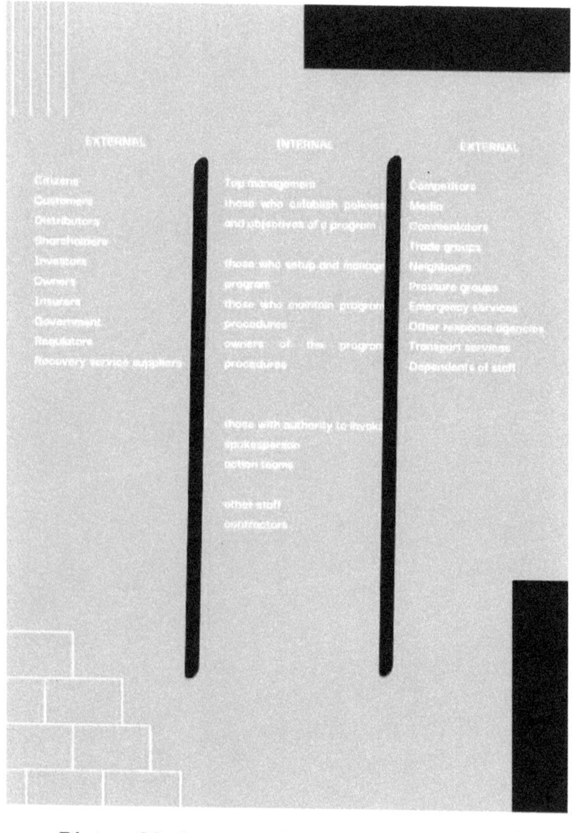

Picture39: Interested Parties (ISO 22313)[6]

[6] Dame Vivian Hunt, Robin Nuttall, and Yuito Yamada, *"From principle to practice: Making stakeholder capitalism work"* , Mckinsey & Company- Article, April 26, 2021

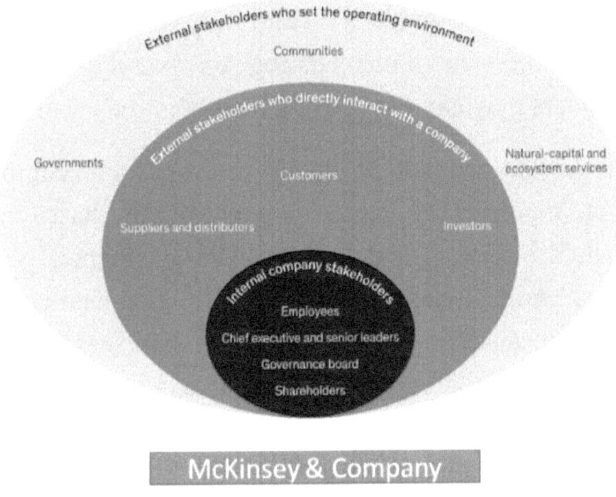

Picture40: Interested Parties (McKinsey)

Many management systems expect that the Interested Parties and their needs and expectations are captured. In my audit experience (across companies and countries), this is a common weak area/ ignored area or the common improvement opportunity (I am not classifying this as major/ minor non-conformity yet).

I had found the ISO 22313 diagram very meaningful and useful. A little from the McKinsey paper also makes more sense:

"Admittedly, the categories are not as clear-cut as this suggests. Governments can be customers, too. An employee can also be an investor, a consumer, and a resident of the local community. And the environment is everywhere. That said,

---

,https://www.mckinsey.com/business-functions/strategy-and-corporate-finance/our-insights/from-principle-to-practice-making-stakeholder-capitalism-work

these categories provide a useful way to think about the subject; moreover, understanding the varying roles that stakeholders play can give deeper insight into their needs.

Not all stakeholders will be equally relevant for all companies, so it is important to decide where to start, based on the company's business model and values. A financial-services company might choose to prioritize financial-capability building because it is embedded in that sector and has expertise. An oil refinery, on the other hand, might decide to prioritize operational impact and therefore choose to address the local environment, such as air quality, traffic, or emissions."

The above examples for a financial company and an oil refinery help to understand why management systems accord so much importance to this seemingly insignificant activity.

I would like to add one more. Green Peace is an interested party to all Organisations not in good times though. But in bad times. Not in all bad times e.g. financial scam or sexual harassment may not be their concern. But a fire that creates smoke and damages the environment Green Peace is the most interested party for all Organisations. Similarly, Green Peace is more significant interested party to industries that pollute more (relatively) e.g., cement, petrochemicals, power (thermal/ coal) etc.

You may also like to watch my video post on my YouTube channel or for many more informative videos.[7]

---

[7] www.youtube.com/damandevsood*https://www.youtube.com/watch?v=q45dLiIC5kc&t=1s*

13 Journey from RM (Risk Management) to GRC (Governance, Risk, and Compliance) to IRM (Integrated Risk Management) to OR (Organisational Resilience)

While Risk domain is very old, Governance and Compliance added in past decade or so, many Organisations still do not have the Risk Function/ department. Some have reactive approach to Risk Management. Rarely, one has the list of regulatory requirements, and almost no one has the process to establish the same. Even in the Organisations that have very well-established Risk function/ department, the methodology for Risk Management is not documented. And finally, where you find the methodology, then the methodology and the output do not match. This way, a lot of improvement exists in the full ecosystem.

I know almost the whole world claimed that they were almost 100% work from home during Covid-19 Pandemic, I believe both parties - the suppliers and the customers have made an unsaid/ unsigned compromise. I believe the home cannot match the office with respect to physical or information/ cyber security. Somehow, I have not been able to digest a situation where we are in an online session (meeting/ training) and the cameras are not on that simply brings the effectiveness down. Why should we use the platforms like zoom, Microsoft Teams, Cisco WebEx, Google Meet etc., if camera is not to be switched on?

I believe there is no perfect solution. Whether we talk of GRC or BCM or Organisational Resilience as a whole, the most important point is that 'it's all about people'which to my next belief is the weakest link in the chain. Some provisions like NDA, Code of Conduct/ Ethics, Whistle Blower Policy, Information Security Policy, Clear Desk Policy etc. help. Work from home dilutes it further. Most of these are 'one time signed and forgotten' documents. Regular reminders and re-enforcement are required.

The first point is 'not to be a pigeon' (in a mythological story, the pigeon closes its eyes when it sees cat as if there was no risk) i.e. as a COO, I would first like to admit that I have these challenges, only then I have a possibility of resolving these (or at least some of these). While some tools do help, access rights can also control the situation to an extent. Overall, manual audits cannot be replaced. Sometimes, setting an example helps e.g. disciplinary action on one employee will set the rest right for long.

I have been practicing Risk Management for over 30 years, a lot has changed with respect to my own understanding as well. I started using the principles of ISO 31000 in last 10 years or so. The key in Risk Management is to be able to understand the context of your own Organisation (trust me, many do not), based on which one would do the identification - for which I have expanded my sources including brainstorming, books, summits/ conferences, webinars, AON maps, WEF (World Economic Forum) Global Risk Report, other Horizon Scanning Reports etc.

I develop a Heat Diagram to sort the risks, and the top (hot) ones become my target. Metrics are difficult. Theoretically Return on Investment (RoI), Cost Benefit Analysis, Payback period etc. can be used. But mostly this has been qualitative and hence has been subjective.

There is constant eye on existing and emerging risks locally, nationally, and globally. Then regular meetings are held to review the whole elements risk management process, parameters, definitions, risk appetite, effectiveness of the controls, progress on in-implementation controls (some risks will take long to get mitigated e.g. training 15000 people may be yearlong program).

My audit experience is that 'almost everyone knows Risk Appetite, but no one knows it actually'. People tell me the definition. I am not interested in definition the question is about 'your risk appetite'. Even if the value is known, it is known only to few people. Even those people then do not use it. And the value is too old (not reviewed/ refined in recent times). Ultimately, I would like to see the process (documented process written, reviewed, approved, published, used) to establish the risk appetite.

This is a long and continuous journey. Even large and matured Organisations that I have interacted with during my training and consulting assignments (and I have touched hundreds and hundreds of them) lack at this point. The most that they do is first level of risk management. I tend to go deep and to many levels lower than that. Covid-19 Pandemic is a good example.

The risk of Covid-19 was managed (by the governments) by announcing lockdowns. This created another risk for the Organisations they managed it by work from home (mostly). But that gave rise to multiple risks – physical security, information security, infrastructure, stress, sedentary lifestyle, privacy etc. During 6 months of Covid-19 Pandemic, I have run over 60 mini surveys with one common question "are you eagerly looking forward to going back to office' and the responses have been from 45%-55% 'yes' (touching 100% in couple of cases). My interpretation is that 'there is some pain' at home!

In one of the discussions with me, the CEO of an Organisation said, "Daman, I agree, we perhaps have been working from home 'illegally'".

Simple approach of identify-evaluate-mitigate works well. A degree of qualitative and quantitative parameters exists in this. I have been following principles defined in ISO 31000 as a whole Risk Management Process. I know ISO 31010 also exists and has over 30 techniques just for Risk Assessment, but I have not used those yet.

In recent times (added challenges by the Covid-19 Pandemic), I see transformation of roles COO-to-CEO. No emotions, just being reasonable and practicable. There are pressures on revenues and profits. I see emergence of highly Resilient Organisations.

Risk Management, Governance Risk and Compliance came closer decade ago. There have been discussions about Integrated Risk Management or Integrated Management Systems some successes have been achieved - mostly ISO 9001, ISO 14001, ISO 45001 (Quality Management System, Environment Management System, Occupational Health and Safety Management System).

ISO 22316:2017 related about 20 domains/ disciplines to Organisational Resilience, and I see it to be exceedingly difficult to integrate so many into one! I have recently developed a 2-days course on Organisational Resilience (based on ISO 22316) will talk about it separately. And, in the process I realized need for a tool to Assess the Organisational Resilience and developed one while doing this I added 4 more parameters, and this assessment now revolves around 24 factors.

In the immediate terms, I see the transformation from RM-GRC-IRM to OR (Organisational Resilience). The world is going through difficult times. The CxOs need to take some tough decisions. Multiple domains need to amalgamate. Hence, I see Organisational Resilience to be the solution. The need of the hour is to be more efficient to generate resources (including budget) to invest in tools, techniques, people and be Resilient.

My definition: **A Risk Managing, Learning, and Continually Improving Organisation is a Resilient Organisation!**

14 United Nations SDGs and Organisational Resilience

The whole book is providing you an opportunity to understand the Big Why of Organisational Resilience. This chapter in particular asks to implement Organisational Resilience from the point of view of supporting and committing to the UN SDGs (Sustainable Development Goals). Refer Picture 27 UN SDGs.

Are you a progressive, forward-looking Organisation, committed to UN SDGs?

Then implementing Organisational Resilience is the way forward!

The United Nations' 17 Sustainable Development Goals (SDGs) aim to achieve decent lives for all on a healthy planet by 2030.

First impression is that Organisational Resilience supports all those goals. Here, I am attempting to write few that I believe are closer to Organisational Resilience. I will attempt to put these in the order to significance (my views).

9. Industry, Innovation, and Infrastructure - Build **resilient** infrastructure, promote inclusive and **sustainable** industrialization, and foster innovation

11. Sustainable Cities and Communities - Make cities and human settlements inclusive, safe, **resilient, and sustainable**

2. Zero Hunger End hunger, achieve food security and improved nutrition and promote **sustainable** agriculture

6. **Clean Water and Salinization** - Ensure availability and **sustainable** management of water and sanitation for all

7. **Affordable and Clean Energy** - Ensure access to affordable, reliable, **sustainable,** and modern energy for all

8. **Decent Work and Economic Growth** - Promote **sustained**, inclusive, and **sustainable** economic growth, full and productive employment, and decent work for all

12. **Responsible Consumption and Production** - Ensure **sustainable** consumption and production patterns

15. **Life on Land** - Protect, restore, and promote **sustainable** use of terrestrial ecosystems, **sustainably** manage forests, combat desertification, and halt and reverse land degradation and halt biodiversity loss

16. **Peace, Justice, and Strong Institutions** - Promote peaceful and inclusive societies for **sustainable** development, provide access to justice for all and build effective, accountable, and inclusive institutions at all levels

17. **Partnerships for The Goals** - Strengthen the means of implementation and revitalize the global partnership for **sustainable** development"

14. **Life Below Water** conserve and **sustainably** use the oceans, seas, and marine resources for **sustainable** development

1. **No Poverty** end poverty in all its forms, everywhere

3. **Good Health and Well-Being** ensure healthy lives and promote well-being for all at all ages

4. Quality Education Ensure inclusive and equitable quality education and promote lifelong learning opportunities for all

5. Gender Equality - Achieve gender equality and empower all women and girls

10. Reduce Inequalities - Reduce inequality within and among countries

13. Climate Action - Take urgent action to combat climate change and its impacts by regulating emissions and promoting developments in renewable energy

I am not sure whether the UN considered any parameters in ordering these goals, in my re-prioritisation, Climate appears to have come down I do not mean to say that it has less priority. Similarly, Poverty will be eradicated automatically if we become resilient and sustainable through the other goals.

It is just that in this chapter I wanted to focus on **Resilience** and **Sustainability** two that are closest to Organisational resilience.

15 Million Dollars Question-1: So How Resilient Is My Organisation?

First myth to be cleared is that Organisational Resilience is just BCM or Risk Management or Crisis Management or even all three or a few more (ITDR, Information Security etc.) put together. Well, Organisational Resilience is much more than this.

Mark Carroll (a fellow professional, contributed a chapter in my previous book 'My Experiments with ~~Truth~~ BCM') recently linked BIA with medical science BIA is like Triage the patient care or order of care is decided based on the criticality of the patient's condition.

Well, to check the resilience status of your Organisation also you will have to go the medical way. A leading pathological lab is offering the following (listing only 5 out of 16):

1. Primary Health Check
2. Whole Body Check
3. Well Woman Check
4. Senior Citizen Check
5. Platinum Check

Which one do you pick and how? You can have your own guesses (based on your own assessment of your health), or you go by what he/ she (medical) consultant recommends.

First look tells doctor if something is wrong. I visited a doctor with my brother who had suddenly started feeling difficulty in speaking. Couple of sentences and the doctor opined of a stroke, and then advised MRI that confirmed the same. And then the treatment was started.

But first looks may be good (and deceptive) - the doctor asks you couple of questions. Starts touching you pulse, BP, SPO2 (we all know this now, thanks to Covid-19 Pandemic), temperature etc. and starts forming some opinion.

And these may be followed by many more diagnostics and consultations, sometimes with many specialists before an opinion about your health is firmed up and then the treatment is recommended.

This reminds me of another of my own story. Another brother felt chest pain (suddenly no previous complaints), I rushed him to the hospital Emergency driving myself (did not want to wait for the ambulance). The doctors looked at both of us walking into the Emergency and laughed 'this is emergency, who is the patient out of you two (both looked happy, healthy)?'. Then they ran an ECG on my brother and immediately took him into triage, then the angiography and angioplasty done within next couple of hours.

The same could be done for you for your Organisational Resilience.

Yes, this is human psychology no one wants to admit that he/ she has some problem "I am happy-healthy/ I have never had any problem etc. etc. If I go to the doctor he/ she will sure find out something wrong". Trust me, no symptoms do not mean 'no challenge' a periodic health check-up is strongly recommended. Same is the case about the Organisations also. Organisations believe that they have good systems in place and that they have been doing well revenues and profits are only two of the performance parameters there are 20 more (approximately).

Organisations that have been established for long, need it more inefficiencies creep in overtime and need attention/ resolution!

16 Million Dollars Question-2: Do CEOs Play Any Role in Organisational Resilience?

The answer is a commonsense answer – Top management's continued commitment is the most critical success factor for any program in any Organisation.

(the following points are based on portions from Texas Medical Center president and CEO Bill McKeon's interview with McKinsey)

- CEOs must touch everyone on the frontlines, to really understand how they see the world, how they see the culture of the company.
- On the contrary CEOs put too many layers between them and the frontlines and they lose the real beauty of the Organisation.
- CEOs must de-layer as much as they possibly can
- Get as close to the frontlines of business.
- Make sure the people on those frontlines are treated as well as any other person in the executive suite.
- They will know a culture, you cannot fake it.
- Not something that you put on the wall in a coffee room.
- It is what you live every day.
- Your conduct must not make them consider themselves on the lowest levels of importance.
- The culture of the company should be inclusive of all people in the company.
- It takes time.
- Company without great culture will never perform admirably.

When I deliver a training (in person/ classroom training), I move a lot making direct eye contact with participants, asking questions, and responding to their queries. I call it 'going deep in the problem – to find its solution' – This is a great trait that all CEOs must possess, display, and execute – in BAU and in Crises.

17 Organisation's Purpose and Resilience

Who Will Cry If You Die – wrote someone.

There is another version – for the companies - "What would the world lose if your company disappeared?"

The answer lies in the 'purpose' (or the Vision statement) of the company.

It defines a company's core reason for being and its resulting positive impact on the world. Winning companies are driven by purpose, reach higher for it, and achieve more because of it. Competitors wonder where they can get some of that magic and how they might sprinkle it on.

It was 'eye-washing' long ago, then we learnt 'green-washing' 12 years ago, and today it may be 'purpose-washing'!

A superficial approach to purpose doesn't work. In fact, it can do considerable harm, opening up your company to accusations of inauthenticity or "purpose-washing," turning off customers or driving them away completely, and disaffecting employees up and down your Organisation. Poor outcomes follow when purpose is a patch job.

At Unilever, brands with purpose grew 69% faster than the rest. Indeed, purpose may become essential to future profit as consumers become increasingly conscious of the social and environmental impacts of their purchases. Alan Jope, the company's CEO, recently announced that "in the future, every Unilever brand will be a brand with purpose."

Another article titled "Purpose, or 'purpose- washing'? A crossroads for business leaders"[8] helps to understand the linkages much better.

Seven clear themes emerged from the conversations held with 45 of the world's leading CEOs:

1. In the long run, there is no tradeoff between profit and purpose
2. Purpose begins with your employees
3. Purpose drives innovation
4. A company's purpose must be authentic and embedded in corporate DNA
5. 'Proof points' along the way will help create credibility
6. A strong commitment to purpose helps you make decisions when times turn tough
7. Millennials and Generation Z are driving change

Out of the above number1, 2, 3 are my favourites. Also, good to read what Intel CEO Bob Swan said about point 6 "When the shit hits the fan—whether it is COVID or social injustice—we look to our purpose to figure out what to do".

---

[8]Alan Murray, Bruce Simpson, *"Purpose, or 'purpose- washing'? A crossroads for business leaders"*, November 12, 2020 available at- https://finance.yahoo.com/news/purpose-purpose-washing-crossroads-business-220000567.html

18 Empower Your Employees for Better Decision Making

Who doesn't want to make better, faster decisions? Easier said than done, of course; McKinsey research shows that executives, on average, spend almost 40 percent of their time making decisions and believe most of that time is poorly used.[9]

The opportunity costs are staggering: for the average Fortune 500 company, they typically equal more than half a million days of managers' time, or $250 million a year in salaries.

[9] Aaron De Smet, Caitlin Hewes, and Leigh Weiss, *"For smarter decisions, empower your employees"*, Mckinsey & Company, September 09, 2020 available at- https://www.mckinsey.com/business-functions/people-and-Organisational-performance/our-insights/for-smarter-decisions-empower-your-employees

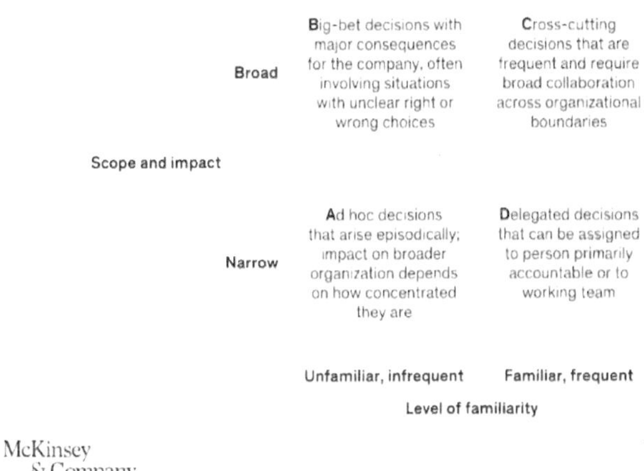

Picture41: McKinsey11

Fully empowered employees make good decisions and resolve problems.

Easier said than done – McKinsey recommends few steps also:

1. Ensure that your Organisation has a well-defined, widely understood strategy.
2. Clearly define roles and responsibilities. (I add 'authorities' also).
3. Invest in capability building (and coaching) up front.
4. Build an empowerment-oriented culture.
5. Decide when the other managerial archetypes are appropriate.

When it comes to decision making, there is a saying 'analysis paralysis' is not good. I have written in an earlier chapter 'take a decision and own it'. You may also like to say, 'decide to decide'. Actions are important. We may realize that a good delivery on time would be appreciated more than a better delivery on missed commitments.

This is how an Organisation is built resilient.

19 Invest in intangibles and grow more!

An intangible asset is an asset that is not physical in nature. Goodwill, brand recognition and intellectual property, such as patents, trademarks, and copyrights, are all intangible assets. (Investopedia)

Companies that master the deployment of intangibles investment will be well positioned to outperform their peers.[10]

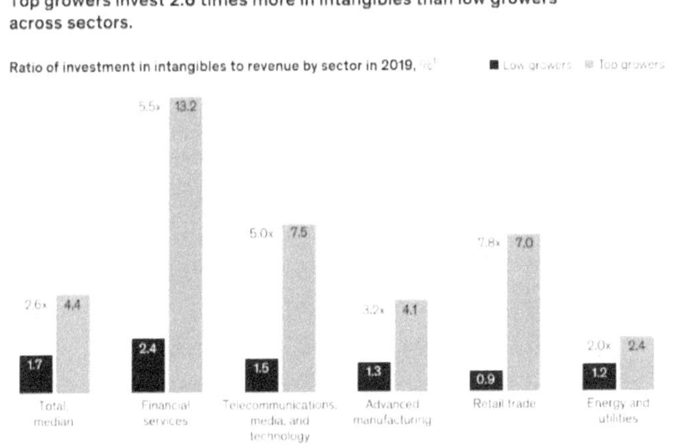

Picture42: McKinsey12

---

[10] Eric Hazan, Sven Smit, Jonathan Woetzel, Biljana Cvetanovski, Mekala Krishnan, Brian Gregg, Jesko Perrey, and Klemens Hjartar, "*Getting tangible about intangibles: The future of growth and productivity?*", Mckinsey & Company, June 16, 2021 available at- *https://www.mckinsey.com/business-functions/growth-marketing-and-sales/our-insights/getting-tangible-about-intangibles-the-future-of-growth-and-productivity*

Innovation, idea generation are key to IP. Brand management is equally important.

But do your employees understand this? Without this understanding how will they contribute effectively to the progress of the Organisation?

I teach that collaboration between various functions and breaking the silos helps to move towards that common goal – the 'Purpose' – the force that keeps all bound together.

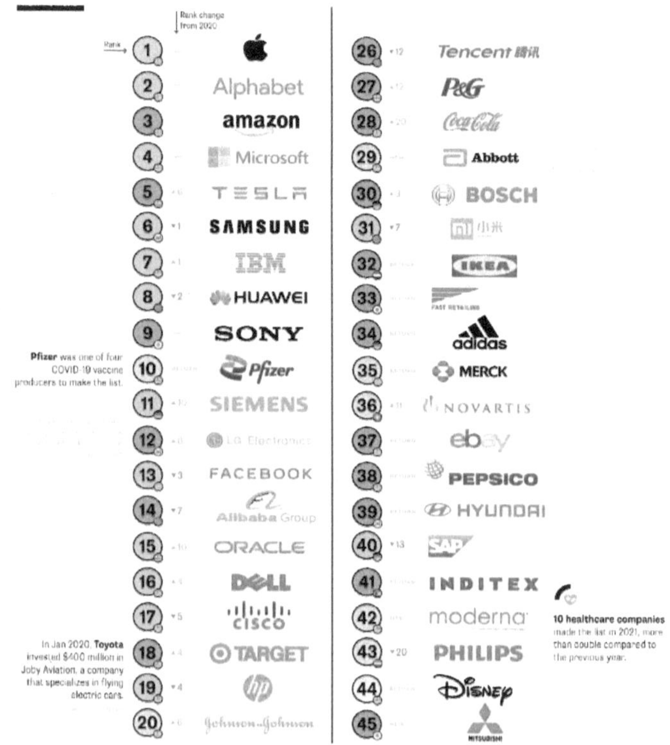

Picture43: Most Innovative Companies[11]

Apple and IBM were top companies in 2021 with respect to number of innovations and number of patents granted – I guess there are no doubts that these are resilient companies.

While on some point, I have dislike about Apple – that it does not produce sustainable products i.e. the feelings are as if the product is programmed to start malfunctioning (major fault) as soon as its out of warranty – debatable, I am sure.

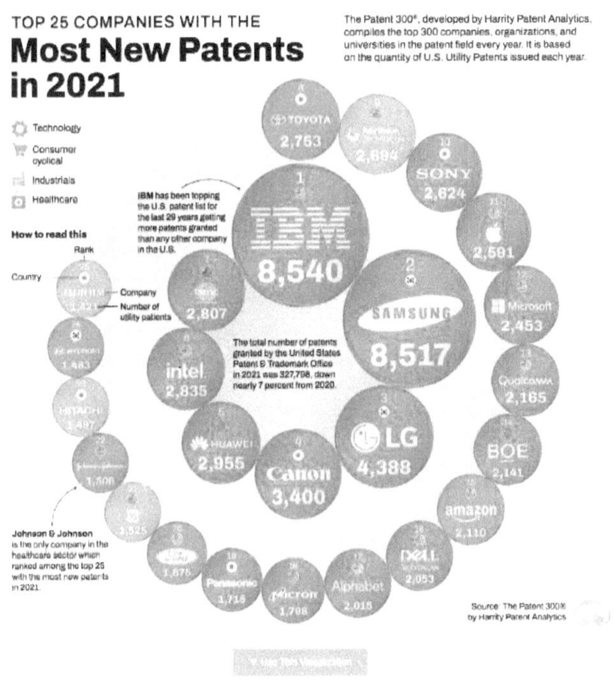

---

[11] https://www.visualcapitalist.com/ranked-the-most-innovative-companies-in-2021/

Picture44: Most Patents for Companies[12]

(The above two infographics have been produced with thanks and permission of Visual Capitalist. I understand that they have updated versions of these pictures, but I do not expect them to be too different from the above).

[12] *Visualizing Companies with the Most Patents Granted in 2021 available at-https://www.visualcapitalist.com/visualizing-companies-with-the-most-patents-granted-in-2021/*

20 HR and Organisational Resilience

The following pictorials taken from a McKinsey article help to understand 'Why HR Leaders Want to Focus On People Again'.

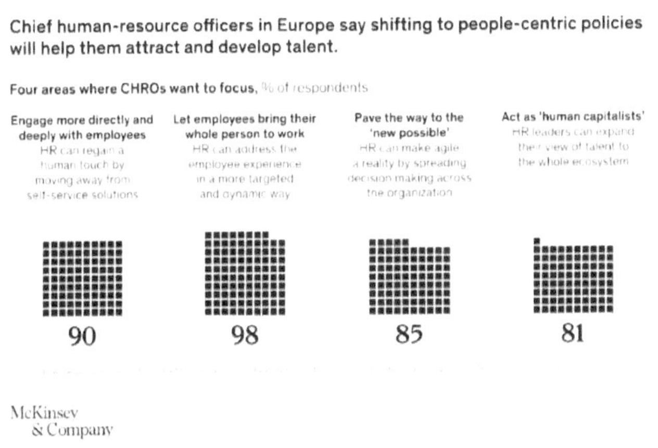

Picture45: McKinsey13[13]

[13] Talha Khan, Asmus Komm, Dana Maor, and Florian Pollner, "'Back to human': Why HR leaders want to focus on people again", Mckinsey & Company, June 04, 2021 available at- *https://www.mckinsey.com/business-functions/people-and-Organisational-performance/our-insights/back-to-human-why-hr-leaders-want-to-focus-on-people-again*

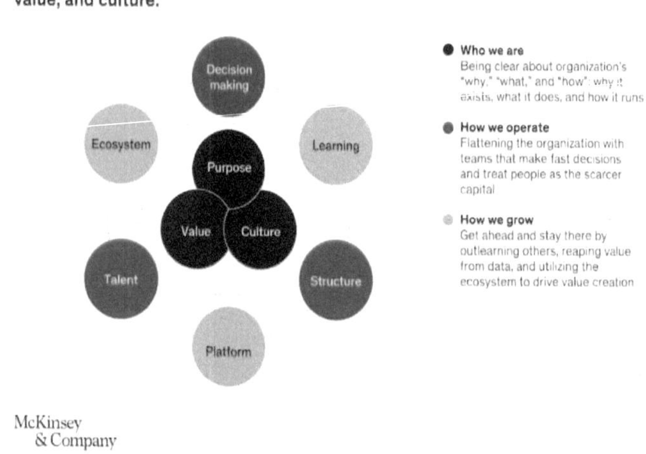

Picture46: McKinsey14

Direct and deep engagement with people is recommended – we start getting a feeling that to be a resilient company we would have to take care pf our people hence HR plays a big and important role in developing Organisational Resilience.

I have written about decision making elsewhere in the book. We may like to call it Agile Decision Making now after the extended Covid-19 Pandemic period.

21 Sleep and Be Resilient!

The infographic below depicts the loss of sleep according to a McKinsey article.

- One in three Americans does not get enough sleep
- Globally, up to 45 percent of the population doesn't get enough sleep
- Loss of deep sleep is
  - Linked to a long list of chronic health conditions, including Alzheimer's disease, anxiety, dementia, depression, hypertension, and type 2 diabetes
  - It also affects cognitive function, attention, and decision making
- Sleep deprivation carries high economic costs
  - $680 billion a year in five OECD countries
    - $400 billion for the United States
    - $60 billion for Germany
- Direct and indirect cost of sleep disorders in Australia equals 1 percent of GDP.
- Sleep-related absence from work results in loss of
  - 10 million working hours a year in the United States
  - 4.8 million working hours in Japan
  - 1.7 million working hours in Germany
- Lost sleep also reduces productivity
  - Annual cost at $1,300 to $3,000 per employee in the United States
- Lost sleep also raises healthcare costs for employers

Picture47: McKinsey15

I link this to 'Personal Resilience' which is in line with 'Organisational Resilience'.

I stress upon people care. But should employers be worried about employees' sleep? Yes, if you believe you have done everything else in the name of people engagement and development then this is your continual improvement.

And technology can help - In the United States, the number of sleep-technology patents has increased by an average of 12 percent a year over the past decade.

Market forecasts indicate that the resulting influx of sleep devices could take the global market to some $32 billion by 2026, up from $11 billion in 2019. Many of the new devices focus on monitoring the quality of sleep, motion, and biosignals and therefore open up the possibility of accurately monitoring sleep at scale for the first time.

So, are you getting an idea about your next startup?

22 Technology and Ethics

Technology is great enabler to Resilience, but we must not forget the Ethics!

The world has been going through perhaps the longest crisis of history i.e. Covid-19 Pandemic (yes, it is not over yet!).

As an expert in the Resilience domain (Organisational Resilience, Business Continuity Management, Risk Management, Crisis Management etc.), I would like to submit that no one (yes, no one) in the world was prepared for this Pandemic – the way it happened.

In near memory, we would not be able to recall – offices being locked due to a disease. Not ALL OFFICES ALL AROUND THE CITY/ STATE/ COUNTRY/ GLOBE could be locked due to a pandemic – but it happened.

So, an immediate, short term (Organisations hate to admit this) measure was taken – 'work from home'. Almost everyone across globe worked from home, almost all Organisations claimed 100% productivity also.

My views, once again, are based on my global experience of last 16 years of having been a practitioner, trainer, consultant, auditor of Business Continuity Management.

I have run over 100 surveys in last 20 months (at the time of writing this chapter) or so – covering over 1200 people from countries and companies, all genders, all ages, all professions etc. A long report is available separately – 'work from home' is a solution but not a permanent solution, not a long-term solution. It has multiple challenges associated with it – and I present those in my study.

In this discussion, I will just focus on one point i.e. the risk/ challenge of ethics.

Technology was exploited to make 'work from home' work. It included providing secure platforms, virtual working tools (zoom, Microsoft Teams, Cisco Webex, Gotomeetings etc. – improved tremendously and at the speed of light).

Let us first look at the definition of Ethics (from internet):

- The study of what is right and wrong in human behaviour
- Beliefs about what is morally correct or acceptable

My simple way is 'doing what I am supposed to do' is ethical. This would not have changed over millions of years. But some expectations are more important today e.g.

1. Taking care of the environment
2. Working towards Sustainability and Environmental Sustainability
3. Reducing carbon footprint
4. Reducing, reusing, recycling
5. Ensuring CIA (confidentiality, integrity, availability) of information/ data
6. Taking care of people (the greatest asset – buildings and IT are only secondary)

I have not been able to dig the exact figures – how many IT devices were there in the world at end of 2019, and how this figure has changed by the end of 2020. But I believe that it is safe to assume at least 100% increase during this period. While there are many IT devices, but we could easily focus on the big items like laptops, desktops, printers.

Now let us attempt to see how 'work from home' – highly supported by technology has impacted these 6 areas (there could be many more, I am just looking at these 6):

Taking care of the environment – we have mined more to produce more. We have consumed more to manufacture more. We have more because of more. All this is against the above common sense/ need of the hour/ ethical activities.

Our carbon footprint has increased for sure – due to this increased mining, increased manufacture, and increased usage. So, are we on the path of Ethics?

These IT equipment are going to produce more e-waste (which already was a big challenge) in couple of years – do we have enhanced capacity for safe disposal/ **recycling of these**. I guess neither the manufacturer nor the user has thought of this (they may say they did not have time – the need was to ensure continuity – 'work from home' for many more people). **So, this is not sustainable development** and also is not ethical once again.

I also believe that both the customer and the vendor have done some compromises while working from home – compromise in physical security, information security, physical health, mental health etc. So, technology came to rescue, but resulted in unethical way of working. There, for sure, is a compromise on **CIA of data/ information**.

This point is very serious – did we **really take care of our people**? I have been advocating an Emotional Impact Assessment* – did we ask the employee whether he/ she wanted to work from home? Are we asking them now whether they want to go back to 'work from office'? Last year a sense of 'us and they' got created – most people were working from home (safe place) while some had to be in the office (essential services/ type of activity etc.) – which was not considered to be safe. So, those working in the office started developing a feeling that they were 'unlucky'/ their lives were not precious. So, did the managements work Ethically?

A professional associate from UK recently (at the time of writing this chapter) mentioned, that there was a feeling that 'we are being forced to go back to office' while UK has started opening up– this should not be ignored.

Technology was great rescuer – the next question that comes to mind is about the huge additional infrastructure (desktops, laptops, routers, desks, printers etc.) that has been created – what happens to it when the offices open again? Its unethical to leave at homes as it is company property or how will finance write it off? If the whole infrastructure is taken back to the office – then there is no space for it in the office (most likely).

In conclusion, I believe Technology (as in the past) has been helpful during Covid-19 management (I am not talking about medical side of it) also, but this has increased Ethical Pressures, and the works is far from over.

And, if we have not taken care of these (increased medical and electrical waste) then none of us can claim to be resilient yet.

23 Role of Emotional Impact Assessment in Organisational Resilience

I have stressed enough on need to take care of people as resilient people make resilient Organisations. Hence this long chapter on Emotional Impact Assessment (EIA). If you get a feeling of this being in the form of question-answer session, then you are right this is based on an interview session where given questions were put to me.

Many people will recognise EIA as Environmental Impact Assessment done during ISO 14001 implementations, but the EIA I have been talking about is Emotional Impact Assessment. This is also different from the BIA that we conduct in BCM. In ISO 14001, the Environmental impact is while the process has been running; in BIA, the impact is when the process has come down. This Emotional Impact Assessment is when some incident/ disaster has happened, and the process is running but in recovery mode.

I had the routes of the Emotional Impact Assessment rooted way back in 9/11 – actually couple of years later when I came to know of this incident. A husband-wife used to see the twin towers daily from their window. On the day, the wife knew that the husband had to be in one of those towers for a meeting, and by chance she saw the first plane hitting the tower live from her window. Just this thought that the husband could have been there – she went mad for 5 years! The husband did not go there, the meeting was cancelled due to some reason, he came home in the evening happy-healthy, but it took wife 5 years to recover. There would be many such cases that are not even recorded anywhere – because she was not one of those present in the towers or directly impacted.

Many times, you would have been driving and would have seen an animal ahead on the road already crushed by some vehicle – your hands shake – what if it were a person – a friend, family member or colleague – not dead – but dying?!

Then this started agitating me more during Covid-19 Pandemic when the issues started surfacing like – number of home violence have gone up, number of divorces have gone up, more number of people are seeking counselling – that means there are some pains of working at home, there is stress – and now emotional impact assessment is needed more than ever before – not financial impact, not reputational, legal or operation impact but what is the emotional impact of a crisis? Some Organisations might have started providing some services now that the Pandemic has continued for long, but I believe no one ever thought of this.

Companies just made the arrangements for their employees to work from home – what was the condition at home no one bothered to ask (they did not have any option either) – whether there was one or 2-5 people working from home, who will work from where? Family members, kids, parents, - not forgetting the pets. All these factors will have an impact on the emotions of a person. I can blindly say that the people have been stressed while working from home – while I have the backing of 68+ surveys conducted globally covering over 1000 people (over 100 surveys covering over1200 people now while finalising this book).

EIA - importance

I believe we can save some time on importance – it should have become clear from the first very long answer. And I would like to keep the second portion short – ultimately its for the Organisation. It will help Organisation to take an informed decision. I know cases where people are eagerly looking forward to going back to office. A sense of 'they and us' is being created. People in UK are feeling that they are being forced to go back to office. All these hint at the need of conducting an assessment of emotional impact of a disaster/ situation/ decision.

Benefits and contributions of a well-performed EIA

It will help Organisations to take informed decisions. People will feel happy that they have been pat of the decision-making process and that their feelings mean a lot to the management. A happy employee is a good employee – the quantity and quality of his/ her output will increase.

The activity may fall under HR, but all units and departments have people, so ultimately all will reap the benefits.

Potential challenges/ issues with performing an EIA

This is human nature – anyone seeking counselling is thought to be a mentally disturbed case. While the perception is changing. This is the biggest issue – due to this people may not like to admit that they are stressed even if they are – and then the results would be skewed.

And also, it may be taken as Employee Evaluation exercise and people may step back. So, communication is the key here.

They need to be taken into confidence first of all. May be this awareness exercise has to reach up to the family members also – so that they encourage their working members to open up.

Performing an EIA, and required tools

This idea is new, I have not performed EIA yet, I do not know anyone who has, So, at this time I have rough ideas.

I believe this is not going to be another impact category in the BIA. Generally, there is no emotional impact of a process going down. Example, payroll process goes down, my salary is delayed – that's all – so some emotions of course, but not to the scale that I would be bothered.

It is the 'incident as a whole' that will cause emotional imbalance – 5 people have died or 500 have fallen sick, or 5000 in the city or 50000 in the country are dead. During Covid-19 Pandemic, 'work from home' became a strategy or solution – but I would like to take this as an incident in my life – and then all those points that we discussed in the beginning – space, desk, machine, connectivity, privacy, family, kids, pets, home violence, divorces, stress, counselling sessions – THIS IS BIG EMOTIONAL IMPACT. This needs to be evaluated.

An article says "The COVID-19 pandemic represents the most universal shared stressor for the general United States (U.S) population in many decades."

Questions asked during EIA

I believe no existing questionnaire can cover this and we need to start from scratch on this front.

A search on PMC7568491 will fetch an example, good starting point.

I ran a Global Emotional Impact Survey; the report is available for free download.[14]

Participants in an EIA

I believe all are human beings, so all can be impacted emotionally and all need to participate in this assessment.

Facilitator/ Performer of the EIA

The one who is strongest emotionally! A funny experience, which is not so funny.

I used to donate blood occasionally, and I used to arrange blood donation camps. As leader, to set example, I would always be the first one to donate. Most of these were in my company where we were able to collect 300-400 units in a day.

Then the great mind wanted to apply Continual Improvement and we thought of setting it up in a big mall – where 20000 footfall was expected in a day. We started at 9am, and by 9:30 I had finished my donation. After that I was roaming around and talking to people and encouraging them to come forward to donate.

A group of young girls came, I talked to them, 1 out of 5 agreed to donate (that is a great success rate!). The doctor and nurse did the initial vitals check and she was found fit to donate. She

[14] *https://www.linkedin.com/posts/damandevsood_global-emotional-impact-assessment-report-activity-6831297680023527424-Il-z?utm_source=linkedin_share&utm_medium=member_desktop_web*

was made to lie on the bed and then the nurse was preparing to insert the needle in her arm, other girls were around the bed and were looking at their friend. This is bit thick needle, you know, while the needle was being pricked, one of the girls looking at her fainted and fell! Do the emotional impact assessment of the situation!

It could have been fatal for the girl who fell! I could have been behind the bars! The donor as well as all her friends perhaps would swear not to donate ever again! Any one around planning to donate could have decided not to donate ever! With word of mouth or news in media – hundreds and thousands more could have decided the same!

Generally, I can say the duration will depend upon survey size also. In an Organisation, invitation must be to all, but we know we will never be able to reach 100% responses, so if they stop at fixed day or at 90% responses in an Employees Satisfaction Survey, they should follow the same for Emotional Impact Assessment as well. But this is just data collection step. Someone good at statistics, someone good at analysis, someone good at human aspects (a counsellor) needs to take it forward to draw meaningful conclusions. I have last two of the three skills. I have designed hundreds of small surveys. Designing surveys is an art – I know it.

Documenting findings of an EIA

It could be a word document report with many different cuts – age wise, position wise, sex wise, location wise. One of my views from India is that 'female employees are looking forward to going back to office more than the male employees'

– strange, isn't it? But it remains a fact – one-on-one interactions with female professionals have yielded this.

Presenting the findings of an EIA

This will be to the top management; HR Head must be present.

Closing remarks

I have moved on from BCM to Organisational Resilience. Resilient People make Resilient Organisations. So, this Emotional Impact Assessment will help us to be more resilient. This will help to take Informed decisions. I hope it will help us to break these myths that

- Work from home is the new norm or
- We will work from home forever or
- A large number of our employees will work from home for long

And to support my view that work from home has more challenges (in terms of emotional impacts) than it solves the challenge – this should be only a temporary solution.

24 BC Plan Testing

BCM (Business Continuity Management) is an integral and important portion of Organisational Resilience, hence I am including this long chapter. BC Plan Testing is an art and needs to be learnt.

Top management's interest/ confidence in BC Tests

Leadership's biggest worry is conformance to the needs and expectations of the interested parties. So, identification of the same is important – we do not even know what do our interested parties expect from us – so how will we meet those expectations.

Their second worry is optimum utilization of the resources, including the budget. So, we need to be reasonable and practicable in our approach to BCM – which is ensured through BIA.

So, these two activities will help in increasing their confidence in the BCMS.

Also, their full involvement in the program will help – no boss, I know you are busy, I will manage, you don't worry – this is not correct – please involve them fully in the program – from policy, to budget, to various approvals, to audits, to tests, to Management Reviews and to the Continual Improvement and for long and forever. All this will increase their confidence in the BCMS.

Communication is important – so the reporting and governance will add to their confidence. That Daman provides inputs without being asked – they should have this confidence. Please do not underestimate the importance of communication in BC Tests – that will add to top management's confidence – I mean good and effective communication will increase their confidence in the BCMS.

And their confidence in their BCMS will go up further with external learnings and sharing – attend – let them know, speak – let them know – write – let them know.

Exercises – I will keep simple and will say Tests – Tests instil the confidence by providing assurance that the plan and the arrangements are effective and will work if and when required. Plan testing also ensures the currency, accuracy, completeness, and effectiveness of the same. People get tired by the time they reach BC plan completion stage and then start taking it easy. But designing, developing, and delivering a BC Test is an art – a lot goes into this.

A simple example is from my coding days – the golden rule was 'catch the defect early, else the cost will be too high' – similarly the BC Plan must be tested as soon as its ready, else it may become a very costly affair if a real incident happens before the test – and we know the disasters don't come knocking at the door with prior approvals!

I noticed this gap in the market and decided to develop this course called 'Design, Develop, and Deliver an Effective BC Test!'

Test design vs BC Plan

I was recently delivering this course (Design, Develop, and Deliver an Effective BC Test) for a major, very well established, and as I have designed the course it was full of hands-on practicals. I asked them to design a Test and could see the number of improvements required in their BC Test approach. One was around this point – you can only test what you have planned – their test plan condition or scenario was not in sync with their BC Plan.

I know a point can be raised that we may face a scenario that we couldn't foresee and hence was not in the Plan – so how will we face it if we restrict ourselves to BC Plan only? Trust me, even if we are able to manage what we could foresee – we are a great Organisation.

All the unforeseen events that the BC Plan/ arrangements will not be able to manage – should be documented in assumptions or limitations of the plan.

Developing a Test

First thing first – it's an art to design, develop and deliver a BC Test. I would again give an example of the coding – while I could do my own testing – unit testing, there were specialized Testers also. Within that, there would be one who would design the test and it had to be according to the requirements and specifications of the code. There would be one who would create the test cases, and there would be one to execute, and one to make observations additionally.

I could write a test that would always pass – skip all the code – just 'start and go to end' - that's not a well-designed test. A code test would have to check basic functionality, as well as the boundaries and exception handling capabilities of the code.

A BC Test will have to have full considerations like

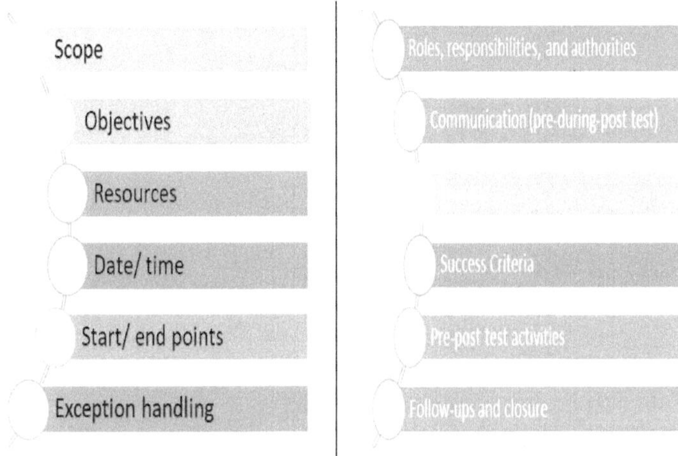

Picture48: BCM Test Considerations

Effectiveness of the BC Tests

Same example of coding – there used to be expected results and actual results. If these match within 10%+- we would claim it to be effective. So, set the criteria in BC Test Plan and measure accordingly.

There will be some quantitative measures, but qualitative measures are equally important. In a simple Test you may like to have 0% deviations from expected results, but please give yourself little space to have deviations in complex tests.

Also, effectiveness of the whole Exercises Program needs to be established.

A quick view may be:

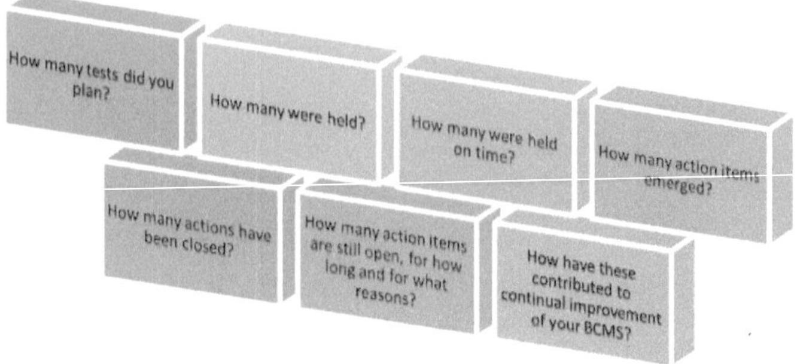

Picture49: Effectiveness of BCM Tests

Tabletop Exercises are not enough.

As good practice, all plans, all people, all arrangements need to be tested over a period. No need to do the most complex test in the beginning, and just continuing to do simple tests is not good either – simple tests involve least complexity, effort, cost, and risk – but are least assuring also.

If I can summarize, based on my experience of having been across companies and countries, many Organisations have many improvements to make:

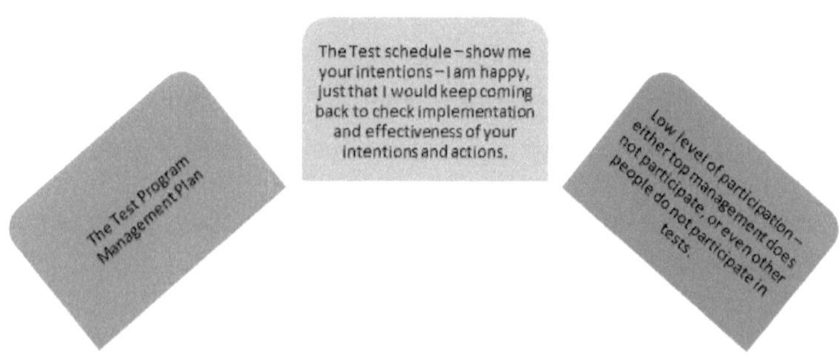

Picture50: Sample Improvements in BCM Tests

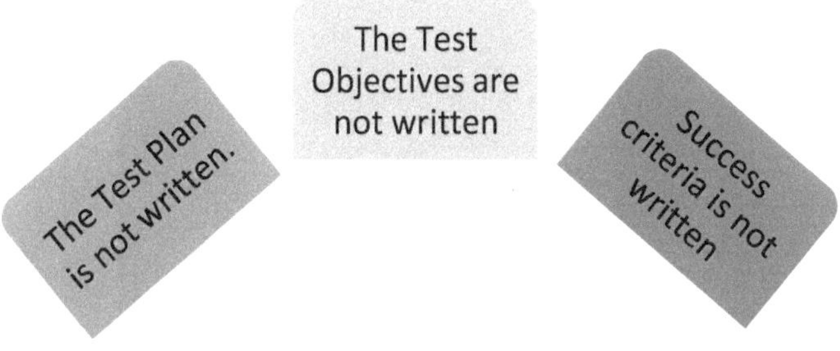

Picture 51

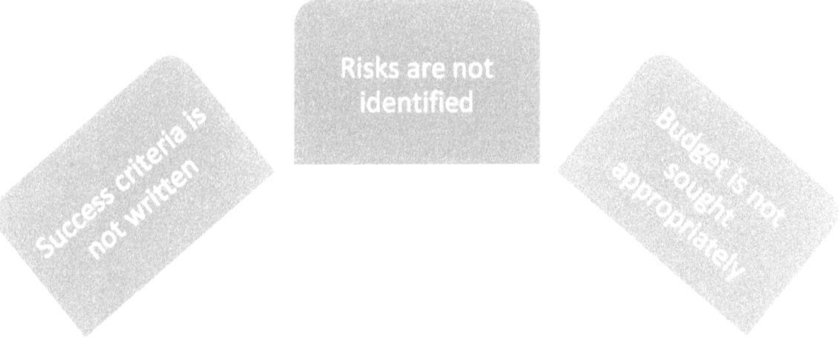

Picture 52

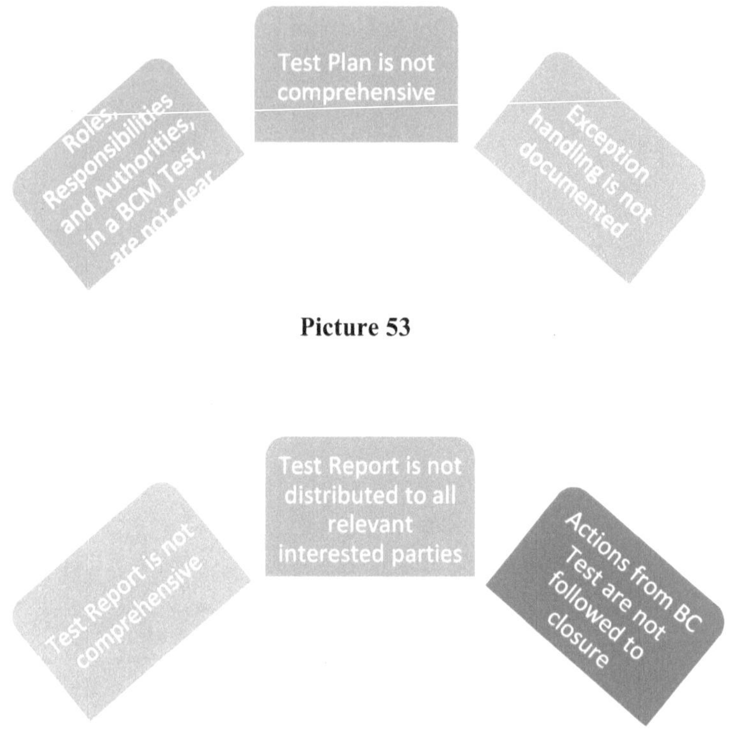

Picture 53

Picture 54

All these refer to the effectiveness of the Test Program, also to the effectiveness of the BCMS, and some also reflect upon the Commitment of the Top Management.

In summary:

How long will your CMT take to approve AED 1.5 million sitting in the Command-and-Control Center?

An Organisation in the UAE took seconds (AED 1.5 million = USD 300000 approximately)!

Are you haunted by any of the following questions regarding a BC Test:

a) Where to start and where to stop a Test?

b) Who all should be involved in a Test?

c) Why should we develop a Test Plan?

d) Who should all participate in a Test/ Who all need to be kept in loop?

e) What all activities need to be conducted in a Test?

f) What is the importance of before-during-and after Test communication?

g) Do vendors/ suppliers/ customers/ regulators play any role on a Test?

h) Should you be running any Tests while 'work from home' is on?

i) How much does it cost to run a Test? What are the budget components?

j) What is the Test cycle?

k) What are different types of Tests? Which one should you be running?

l) Do people know their roles, responsibilities, and authorities in a Test?

m) What should a Test Report contain?

My strong recommendation is that the Organisations attend this course (Design, Develop, and Deliver an Effective BCM Test - for a moment become a learner once again, unlearn to learn – the course has received excellent feedback (including from experts in the field).

Testing (of BCM Plans) is such an important portion in Organisational Resilience that I am happy to extend this chapter to over 10 pages. Here is my input that got included in the BCI BCAW 2022 Exercise Playbook:

10 hot scenarios for you two consider while designing your next BCM Test.

Organisation ABC has allowed hybrid work (office and home) due to the COVID-19 pandemic and expects this to continue for a long period of time. The following 10 cases are realistic and if you crack even 50% of them this year, you would be part of a more resilient Organisation.

Scenario 1: (H2)

There are no guidelines - who can work from home, when and for how long, etc. Therefore, employees are misusing this facility. **Discuss the implications of this scenario**. Bring out all the possible misuses (for example, moonlighting, spending more time with family, accomplishing the work but not being available to others when needed during normal office hours, physical and mental health challenges, etc.)

On investigation, an employee says "we are a bank, and my other work is selling FMCG products online so there is no conflict of interest. I do the other work in my spare time. My work for you is not impacted and you can ask my supervisor. What's your problem?" **Discuss this case**.

Scenario 2: (H2)

The IT staff need to mostly work from an office. Also, if you are a manufacturing unit, shop floor staff need to be in the office while many others (in support functions) can continue working from home. This is creating a 'they-and-us' feeling. Those in the office think that their colleagues working from home are enjoying time with their family while they are at risk (there is a risk of the virus in the office, which is the reason you enabled work from home). **How will you manage this situation?**

Scenario 3: (H2)

Some senior staff have developed a tendency of demanding more work (more than planned work hours) at odd times. Some employees have said that they are logged in almost 24 hours as "you don't know when the boss would write!" This has come through an anonymous mail. **Discuss this situation.**

Scenario 4a: (H2)

You have a whistleblower policy/process. A complaint has come from an employee that their boss has been harassing them by sending undue messages at incorrect times, making demands over phone calls, and focusing on non-office related matters. The person is not able to concentrate on their job and is scared of the implications, with the boss providing some hints. **Investigate the case further. How long will this take in your Organisation?**

Scenario 4b: (H2)

The investigation has established that the boss attempted to make inappropriate advances, including through their own admittance and some material disclosures. The employee complained of mental harassment and disturbances in their family as well. **What is the next step in your process?** Some management members are of the opinion of 'naming and shaming' to set the example, so that others learn their lesson. You have also noticed that there has been an increase in such cases during hybrid working - **what could be fuelling this?**

Scenario 4c: (H2)

The management decided to remove the boss. **Do you have a process to help outgoing employees in finding a new job? Will you support this former employee?** After some time, the HR head has received a request for a background check on this former employee when they are seeking a job with another employer. **What will be your response?**

Scenario 5: (H2)

A husband and wife are both working in your Organisation. They are aware of rules, regulations, and policies (including IT/cyber/password policies). During the hybrid working process, you have refreshed NDAs for all employees, with extra awareness on fraud/cyber security, hardware/software hardening, etc. However, the husband gets lured by someone to exchange some official data for money. He accesses the wife's laptop/account to do this. The case eventually comes to light, as the wife brought this to you. **Discuss the case. What**

actions will you take with regards to the husband? Any actions for the wife?

Scenario 6a: (H2)

One of your employees dies after working from home under hybrid policy/arrangements. The family files for extra compensation, as per 'death on work.' Do you have any such policy for 'death on work'? Is this through company funds or through an insurance company? Will this be a valid claim through the insurance company? Did you get office policies extended to homes? Does your hybrid policy mean office-home or office-anywhere? Will this policy be applicable if an employee dies while working on the road (e.g. a salesperson) or at a coffee shop or virtual office (Regus center, etc.)?

Scenario 6b: (H2)

(Only if there are challenges in paying to this employee's family, for example, if the insurance company denies payment as the policy was for the office). The family takes the case to court. It is in the media as well. The question is 'who allowed the person to work from home without proper policy amendments?' You want to hold a press conference. **Prepare for this and hold the conference.**

Scenario 7: (H2)

A couple (wife in your company, husband with another one – not in competition with you) file for a divorce. They claim working from home created a lot of stress for them. The wife said her day became 36hrs long and there was no support from husband or the family. Husband also admitted to having mental health problems over last 7 months or so. You are a 'best employer award' winner. Employees start voicing this case due to hybrid/work from home situation and begin demanding a full return to office. **How will you manage this situation? Press is also around now – take care of that as well.**

Scenario 8: (H2)

Cyber-attacks and ransomware attacks have increased. You seem to have a feeling that new product details were leaked to a competitor, who then launched the product before you. The Product Head blames this compromise on security due to working from home (no cameras at home, no people around at home, no physical security at home, etc.) **Is it time to revoke hybrid working? Discuss and write an internal mail reasoning your decision.**

Scenario 9: (H2)

Your internal paper on COVID-19 Pandemic Management listed additional expenses last year on account of following:

a) Loss of productivity

b) Cost of lost opportunities

c) Additional medical care for critically sick employees, which was also extended to their families

d) Vaccination for employees, which was extended to their families and then extended to contract staff as well

e) Hardware, software, and connectivity while working from home

f) Physical infrastructure augmentation while working from home

Do you know the figure? Have you accounted for this in your current budget? Will you be able to make similar expenses again if a similar (perhaps worse) situation arises?

Scenario 10: (H2)

You have decided to make a full return to office. Your CEO is a tennis enthusiast and hence the whole company is as well. Inspired by an international player, some of your employees have not and are denying being fully vaccinated. You want to implement a 'no jab – no job' policy. Some employees are saying this is hurting their independence (should be their decision) and disclosure is an intrusion into their privacy. **Discuss the pros and cons and issue an external statement with justification for your decision. Extend the decision to contractors, visitors, and customers (who are also global).**

25 Hybrid/ work-from-home Working Is Not Resilient

Employers are ready to get back to significant in-person presence (that this effort is on for over1 year – tells us that the challenges exist on both sides – in office as well as at home). Employees aren't. The disconnect is deeper than most employers believe, and a spike in attrition and disengagement may be imminent.[15]

My views are different, and, based on over 100 surveys I have conducted globally, I say 'work from home has more challenges than it resolves'. It can be a temporary solution for a number of people – not the long term for a large pool of employees.

Employees are reevaluating their relationships with the employers.

At the same time Employers are underestimating the disconnect and failing to realize that the 'finish line' is a mirage.

IT/ ITeS industry found it to be very easy to shift to work from home/ anywhere, but this industry is struggling both ways and is indecisive – whether to allow its employees continue working from home or to call them back.

---

[15] Aaron De Smet, Bonnie Dowling, Mihir Mysore, and Angelika Reich, *"It's time for leaders to get real about hybrid"*, Mckinsey & Company, June 09, 2021 available at- https://www.mckinsey.com/business-functions/people-and-Organisational-performance/our-insights/its-time-for-leaders-to-get-real-about-hybrid

Physical security, information security, and emotional drains are the biggest dents in Resilience while working from home/ remotely/ anywhere.

My suggestion is to take informed decisions.

26 Organisational Resilience vs BCM!

This question has been put to me many times recently. An easy answer is that BCM is 'one' portion in Organisational Resilience. There are many more portions (up to 20 arguably) in Organisational Resilience.

Organisational Resilience is a journey of transformation. It's like 'cradle-to-grave' (generally thought of while discussing Green IT) story of an Organisation.

I have attempted to show some differences/ comparisons in the following two infographics. These help to show that Organisational Resilience is much more than BCM.

Organisational Resilience v/s BCM

Organisational Resilience	Business Continuity Management
ISO 22316:2017	ISO 22301:2019
This is cradle-to-grave story (20 domains, you may be able to add more yourself)	Just the BCM portion
Collaboration (with interested parties)	No mention
Innovation (ideas to achieve objectives, along with creativity)	No mention
Empowerment (full clause, for decision making and for identifying threats and opportunities)	No mention
Creativity (along with innovation to enhance organisational resilience)	No mention
Relationships (with relevant interested parties)	Only within the BCM organisation – roles/ responsibilities
Vision, Mission, Values, Purpose (lot of focus)	Mission and purpose just touched upon

Organisational Resilience v/s BCM

Culture, attitude, beliefs, behaviours (lot of focus)	No mention
Trusted and respected leadership	Full clause on leadership, but not mention of trust and respect
Coordination, cooperation, coherence, collaboration (between multiple management disciplines)	No mention
Gap assessment (to prioritised tasks and reinforce the concept)	No mention
Demonstrate and enhance (multiple activities)	Only demonstration of top management commitment
Diversity (skills, knowledge, experience, behaviour)	No mention

Picture55: Organisational Resilience v/s BCM

27 Be A Sunflower and Be Resilient!

This anecdote is from a friend Dr. Shiv Dhawan - Thought Leader in strategic management, business continuity management, risk assessment and profit centre operations; Chief of Staff Rhiti Sports Management (P) Ltd.

In his own words.

“”

Life Lesson

This morning as I was having a cup of chai along with soggy rusks (yes I forgot to put them into the airtight container) when a memory popped up.

It was the winter of the year 2000 AD. I was in a field inspection of Dudhwa National Park and was completely pissed off by the high-handed ness of a retired Inspector General of Forests who was on my team and a royal pain in the neck.

I was sitting outside my tent smoking my pipe looking morose when my forest guard Dhondiyal came up. He was 4 months away from retirement and a treasure chest of wisdom. He asked me why I looked as if I had been struck by a meteorite.

I told him my problem and how I didn't know where to turn for support.

He said whenever in doubt always turn to nature for an answer. I loaded my pipe and asked “kaise bandhu?” (tell me how, dear?)

He smiled. And began as you are aware, sunflowers turn according to the position of the Sun. In other words, they "chase the light". But there is another very interesting fact that you probably do not know. Have you ever wondered what happens on cloudy and rainy days when the Sun is completely covered by clouds?

This is an interesting question. Isn't it?

Perhaps you think the sunflower withers or turns its head towards the ground. Is this what crossed your mind?

Well, that's incorrect!

This is what happens:

They turn towards each other to share their energy*!

Nature's perfection is amazing. Now let's apply this reflection to our lives. Many people may become low-spirited, and the most vulnerable ones even become depressed.

How about following the example of the beautiful sunflowers i.e. "Supporting and empowering each other". Nature has so much to teach and guide us.

Let everyone develop a "Sunflower" trait of turning towards each other on their cloudy and gloomy days.

Spread goodness...it will take its natural course.

Sadly Dhondiyal passed away in June 2019 of natural causes, but he did send me a WhatsApp message a week before he departed the planet saying he was sending me a sunflower.

Let's make the world a jannat (heaven) by spending sunflower moments with friends n family n total strangers. Believe me it will cost nothing, but the returns will be phenomenal.

Start right now, and each of us post here on LinkedIn how many sunflower moments we have provided to other needy denizens of this planet.

“”

Picture56: Dads Are Like Sunflowers

My little contribution is that I am spreading the word. Presenting Sunflowers to my known ones – making resilient people to make the planet resilient!

And the infographic above reminds me what my son said on one of my birthdays (when I did not even know Organisational Resilience).

28 Make Bold Innovations Flourish!

In my previous book “My Experiments With BCM”, I have devoted a chapter to “Curiosity, Initiative, Opportunity, and Innovation” where I conclude as “So, keep your curiosity alive, take initiatives, which may provide opportunities and may result into innovations!”

These are part and parcel of Organisational Resilience also.

In a McKinsey article Safi Bahcall, a former biotech CEO, and author of Loonshots*: How to Nurture the Crazy Ideas That Win Wars, Cure Diseases, and Transform Industries,* talks at length about innovation.[16]

Couple of points from his interview:

- As an Organisation grows, the incentives shift from promoting a focus on projects to a focus on politics. You can see it when the conversation around the watercooler changes from ‘my project’ to ‘my career.’
- There is no better way to kill innovation than insisting, ‘Tell me the NPV of your project before you start.’
- Most of the important breakthroughs failed many times before they succeeded. That is where ‘fail fast’ goes wrong. Most companies are too impatient.

---

[16]Erik Roth, *“The Committed Innovator: A conversation with Loonshots author Safi Bahcall”*, Mckinsey & Company, October 11, 2021 available at-, *https://www.mckinsey.com/business-functions/strategy-and-corporate-finance/our-insights/the-committed-innovator-a-conversation-with-loonshots-author-safi-bahcall*

Dr Robert Schuller recommends in his book 'Tough Times Never Last, But Tough People Do' – that we should treat ideas like new babies".

I have picked up the following poem from his book:

Treat them tenderly…

They can get killed pretty quickly.

Treat them gently…

They can be bruised in infancy.

Treat them respectfully..

They could be the most valuable things that ever came into your life.

Treat them protectively…

Don't let them get away.

Treat them nutritionally…

Feed them, and feed them well.

Treat them antiseptically…

Don't let them get infected with the germs of negative thoughts.

Treat them responsibly!

Respond! Do something with them!

Two key words for me here are 'respond' and 'do something with them' – this is where many supervisors/ companies fail, and the ideas fail.

But before responding and doing something with ideas, we need to develop a culture in the Organisation that encourages generation and manifestation of ideas.

I would highly recommend all startups to understand this poem – this will make them resilient!

29 Million Dollars Answer-1

One of the most valuable (and the shortest) chapters in the book according to me, is this.

YOU NEED ONLY ONE REASON TO 'DO' IT – else there are one hundred excuses!

We all can contribute to build Resilient People, which will make Resilient Country, and finally the Resilient Planet.

No more questions on 'Why' of Organisational Resilience.

30 No One Is Perfect in This World!

So, don't even attempt to be one. Being good is good enough (and difficult too) – just be that and keep improving – this is resilience.

Organisational Resilience is also not about being perfect.

I BROKE COVID-19 PANDEMIC PROTOCOL!

There were times earlier last year (2021) when I wore full PPE Kit taking care of critical Covid-19 patient (my brother). But in November 2021 I broke this protocol/ rule.

My brother was a cancer patient and I had been into the hospitals number of times (sometimes twice a week also) but followed all protocols (I used to be the only one with the face shield!) – social distancing would be beyond my control.

My brother lost 8 months long cancer battle on 11th number 2021. We forgot the protocols, while some relatives visited at home (all were wearing mask) and then we took him to Nigambodh Ghat crematorium (those in Delhi will understand) – a very open crematorium, there were rarely any cremations happening (we didn't have good news for ourselves, but good for the rest of the city), we decided to use CNG crematorium (to be environment friendly).

There was a point at hospital (after his death) that I thought of donating his organs to the hospital (but thought that a cancer patient's organs would be of no use) or full body for research. Both would mean either we would get a distorted body or no body at all – this is a great emotional/ sentimental issue still in our society. I did not have courage to discuss this point with his family and we continued with the traditional rituals.

While the crematorium hall was a big space, we had about 35 people – but I did not think of existing protocol in Delhi with respect to gatherings. All were wearing masks – that's it.

Later, we arranged Prayer Meeting – at a Gurudwara (the place of worship for the Sikhs – but its open to all – no restrictions at all) in Sahibabad, Uttar Pradesh (UP). I was not aware of any restrictions in UP, but I did not think of it. Once again, the Gurudwara was a large open space, about 80 people gathered in the hall (which was its normal capacity, I guess, and we might have broken a rule). We ensured this before people entered the hall:

1. All must have a head cover (this is a requirement in Gurudwaras – Covid or no Covid).
2. Anyone who did not have mask – was given a mask.
3. Everyone had to use hand sanitizer.

A token Langar (In Sikhism, a langar is the community kitchen of a gurdwara which serves free meals to anyone and everyone regardless of their background or beliefs such as caste, religion, gender, economic status, or ethnicity.[17]) was also arranged after the prayer (another tradition). The purpose of this meeting and the Langar, I believe, is to make the grieving family feel at ease (and it was visible). This is where people started talking to each other (and the grieving family members. There were hugs also.) and the social distancing might have been compromised once again. People started dispersing in about 30 minutes, but we continued there for about an hour – and this could be another deviation.

The purpose of writing this is to admit that BC/ Resilience is all about people. Preaching (training/ teaching/ consulting) is easier than Practicing. In Hindi, it is articulated as 'Par Updesh Kushal Bahutere!'

I need to practice more!

---

[17] *https://en.wikipedia.org/wiki/Langar_(Sikhism)*

31 Spirituality and Resilience?!

Spirituality and Daman would generally be poles apart! But I still am writing on this topic.

It is understood that Spirituality is misunderstood – it is not necessarily related to religion (which could be my reason of staying away from the same).

Spirituality would generally be linked with the Eastern World, with India specifically more than other countries.

Resilience

Spirituality

Picture57: Resilience and Spirituality

Here is a piece proving that the Western World is also talking of this and talking of this in the corporate world.

(full details in McKinsey article) where Lisa Miller, professor in the clinical-psychology program at Teachers College, Columbia University, and founder and director of the

Spirituality Mind Body Institute has talked about this[18]. In her latest book, *The Awakened Brain: The New Science of Spirituality and Our Quest for an Inspired Life* (Random House, August 2021), Miller reveals that humans are universally equipped with a capacity for spirituality and that our brains become more resilient and robust as a result of it.

"There is in life a power, a consciousness, a dynamism that is greater than human control. When we acknowledge that we are navigating the skies, sailing the high seas, and not controlling life, we make far more profitable, ethical, and sustainable decisions." – she writes. And this is Resilience (personal) according to me – one who is able to make ethical decisions that are profitable on a sustained basis – is a Resilient Person and Resilient People Make Resilient Organisations!

"There's a tendency to feel that a leap of insight, a mystical gain, a dream, a hunch, an intuition, a gut instinct, is somehow not real data. But inner knowing is real data. It's every bit as real as outer data on a piece of paper or on a screen." she continues to add. I do have a disconnection at this point also as I have been saying gut feeling is good, but the better approach is to have a structured approach.

[18] *"Author Talks: How spiritual health fosters human resilience"* Mckinsey & Company, November 23, 2021 available at- *https://www.mckinsey.com/featured-insights/mckinsey-on-books/author-talks-how-spiritual-health-fosters-human-resilience?cid=other-eml-dre-mip-mck&hlkid=0aa0ca6e9c474376b5a777c9e5a35ef5&hctky=12603601&hdpid=4e692858-bce8-4abb-8674-95b6c2f398f1#*

32 Why Do Your Employees Not Understand Your Company's Vision!?

A company's VMV (Vision, Mission, Values) are directly linked to the Organisational Resilience Program.

If I do not understand my company's vision, I will not be able to contribute to it, I will not be able to live to its values! And the Organisation cannot be resilient without the collective contribution of all employees.

The challenge is the way most Organisations do it:

- Leadership goes to an offsite meeting, employs a consultant and the statements are crafted/ drafted.
- These are published on the website and form place in some marketing collateral.

The need is to walk the employees through these statements. If the leadership comes to believe that the employees do not understand the VMV they tend to call for another offsite meeting and go in the above loop.

Picture58: VMV

Following guidelines are based on an HBR article by Sabina Nawaz:

- (lack of communication, she says) Improve communication a mention on website, in a townhall or in a mail is not enough.
- (different altitudes, she says) Resolve 'what's in it for me' puzzle you (the top management) and me (employees at various levels) are on different floors! Come to my level to talk to me.
- (low fidelity, she says) Walk the talk let the employees see actions in line with the bold and beautiful statements.
- (distaste, she says) create the culture where your juniors feel it comfortable to speak up their minds.
- (work avoidance, she says) challenge them to challenge! Aligning to new visions may mean extra work have reward and recognition for those falling in line and act on who do not (but only after you have done the first 4 above!).

33 You Only Have One Heart!

So, you should take particular care of it (and give it to someone very carefully someone that you intend living with for the rest of your life!).

This contribution based on inputs from Vilas Vaidya (an Infosec Risk and Compliance, BCP, DR, freelancing consultant) as his personal experience.

"Just want to share my experience about health facilities in Goa which worked efficiently and saved a life of our school mate who suffered a heart attack.

My classmates from school in Pune decided to have a get together in Doodhsagar, waterfalls, Goa. So I travelled from Bengaluru and the rest of the guys reached from Pune.

To reach Doodhsagar, vehicles typically Sumo, available at station on shareable basis. This service is run only by the villagers, and they take you to a place which is about 30-40 minutes' drive from their stand. After which you need to climb down where you reach the foothills. The falls pours down here and there is a small pond where people can swim. So, some of us decided to take a dip and head back, as you get only 1.5 hours to go the falls and come back.

So, when we started walking, we noticed that one of our classmates was in extreme chest pain below the chest bone, sweating profusely. He was extremely uncomfortable. Discomfort was such that he could neither seat, stand or sleep. Clear indication of heart attack! The entire area is full of rocks.

We shouted to check if any doctor is there in the crowd, there was none. We then decided to check with lifeguards, they came with a stretcher, but our friend could not lie down, finally we used our life jackets as a cushion, so he was in reclined position and started carrying him back.

The path is full of rocks and small rivers, the bridges are narrow so carrying him on stretcher was tricky, but lifeguards were fit and knew their drill, they were short of one person so we had to support and given the age and various ailments almost everyone was having, only two of us could provide the helping hand. I was able to provide support in carrying stretcher but then path is so rocky, there was a fear of slipping and me getting hurt, secondly my shoe sole had come off, so I was not able to keep pace with the lifeguards, luckily there was another more fit classmate helped who helped for some time and then I took over again. On the way back, we met a doctor who asked us to keep rubbing his chest and not let him sleep.

After putting him in the Sumo, we had tough time to keep him awake. There is no mobile signal also for half the distance. Only once you reach a particular spot, you get a signal, we tried calling 108, but the connection was spotty. We thought they understood and so hoping to see the ambulance waiting. There was no ambulance. The driver though knew where the ambulance is parked, it is parked in the police station which was not far away from the stand and took us there directly. After which things moved quickly, doctor / paramedic for the ambulance was close by he came running and we headed to Primary Health Center, Usgaon which is about 1 hour away. He was given sorbitrate, in the ambulance. BP and pulse were monitored.

At Primary Health Clinic, Usgaon, the doctors were very capable and administered all the necessary injections, like Thrombolyser etc. ECG showed he did have a heart attack and had to be shifted to Goa Medical College, closer to Panaji where he was treated well.

The Primary Health Centre also organized Cardiac Ambulance which came round quickly. He now has been brought to Pune and is undergoing further checks and treatment. We are thankful to the lifeguards, the Sumo driver, the ambulance, and the Primary Health Centre for their professional approach. It was good to see that in smaller places, the system worked. None of them asked any money on their own.

The lesson is: We all are aging, so we should be careful in traveling to a place where getting medical help could be tricky. Carry Sorbitrate and Ecospirin with us". (Daman's note: I would still suggest take doctor's advice before consuming).

Upon asking the age group of the group, Vilas responded further "We are all in the age group of 58-61. Many of us are retired or close to retirement. So, people want to get connected and stay connected, thanks to WhatsApp and the likes it has become easy.

Secondly, I would like to add is Heart is a single point of failure. All other organs have a fair amount of resiliency built in, people can survive on one kidney, one lung, one eye and so on. But for heart there is no backup available. People having issues with liver, intestine etc. can lead a good life even if portions are surgically removed, holds good even for the brain to a certain extent. But no such option is available for the heart."

"Also wanted to highlight the importance of DR drills here. The lifeguards and also the ambulance driver, the paramedic in the ambulance appeared well rehearsed. Probably they would have done regular mock drills.", Vilas added further.

So, personal resilience is dependent on this care. Health is Wealth! One way of being resilient is to have good wealth, ultimately, it is the resilient people who make resilient Organisations!

Special thanks to Vilas Vaidya (an Infosec Risk and Compliance, BCP, DR, freelancing consultant).

34 The Curious Case of pre-Existing Conditions in an Insurance Claim

TIMES NATION

SC: Insurer can't refuse med claim citing existing condition

'Proposer Dutybound To Disclose All Facts Within Knowledge'

New Delhi: An insurer cannot repudiate a claim by citing an existing medical condition that was disclosed by the insured in the proposal form, once the policy has been issued, the Supreme Court has said.

A bench of justices D Y Chandrachud and B V Nagarathna also said a proposer is under a duty to disclose to the insurer all material facts within his knowledge.

The proposer is presumed to know all the facts and circumstances concerning the proposed insurance, it added.

While the proposer can only disclose what is known to him, the proposer's duty of disclosure is not confined to his actual knowledge, it also extends to those material facts which, in the ordinary course of business, he ought to know, the court said.

"Once the policy has been issued after assessing the medical condition of the insured, the insurer cannot repudiate the claim by citing an existing medical condition, which was disclosed by the insured in the proposal form and which condition has led to a particular risk in respect of which the claim has been made by the insured," the bench said in a judgment.

The top court was hearing an appeal filed by Manmohan Nanda against an order of the National Consumer Disputes Redressal Commission (NCDRC), rejecting his plea seeking a claim for medical expenses incurred in the US.

Nanda had bought an Overseas Mediclaim Business and Holiday Policy as he intended to travel to the US. On reaching the San Francisco airport, he suffered a heart attack and was admitted to a hospital, where angioplasty was performed on him and three stents were inserted to remove the blockage from the heart vessels.

Subsequently, the appellant claimed the treatment expenses from the insurer, which was repudiated by the latter stating that the appellant had a history of hyperlipidaemia and diabetes, which was not disclosed while buying the insurance policy.

The NCDRC had concluded that since the complainant had been under statin medication, which was not disclosed while buying the mediclaim policy, he failed to comply with his duty to make a complete disclosure of his health conditions.

The apex court said the repudiation of the policy by the United India Insurance company was illegal and not in accordance with law.

It said the object of buying a policy is to seek indemnification in respect of a sudden illness or sickness that is not expected or imminent and that may occur overseas. PTI

Picture59: Times of India News

Some of you might have noticed the news, in the Times of India.

I thought of doing little more. As the case is from the New India Insurance Company, I picked up two others randomly - ICICI Lombard and TATA AIG. And the experience is documented in this long chapter.

I have not been able to conclude what is right/ wrong; have given some recommendation though, but more importantly I look for others' experiences and an opinion from legal experts. I will also be happy if someone from the insurance companies throws more light on the issue.

I believe customers' personal resilience is hurt in such cases - which will have impact on country's resilience (an ultimately will have global impact), hence this attempt to write this curious case!

ICICI Lombard

1. First question is about type of trip (single/ multi trip)

Picture60: ICICI Lombard website1[19]

2. Then the scope of travel (by geography)

[19] General Insurance - Buy Insurance Policy Online in India at ICICI Lombard

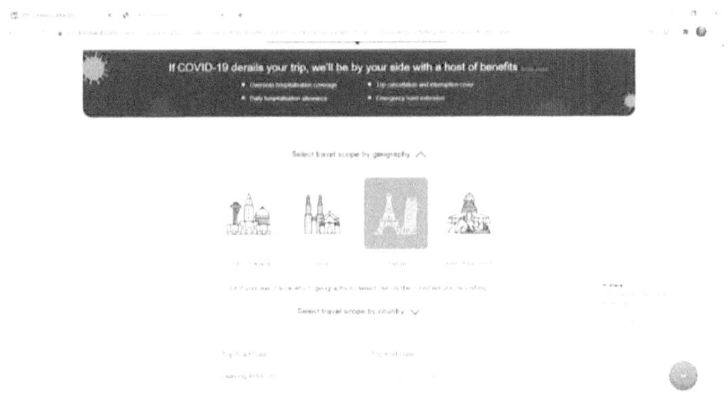

Picture61: ICICI Lombard website2[20]

3. Then the travel dates

Picture62: ICICI Lombard website3[21]

4. Then the number of travelers

[20] *Ibid*

[21] *Supra note 19 at 94*

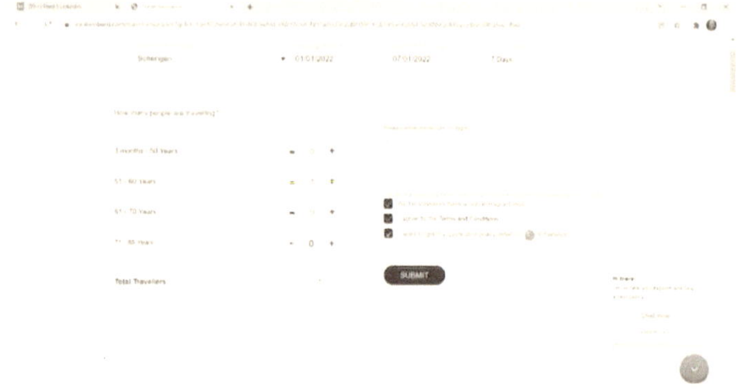

Picture63: ICICI Lombard website4[22]

5. It is mandatory to agree to the terms and conditions but the same are not shown (see above).
6. And the quote is given.

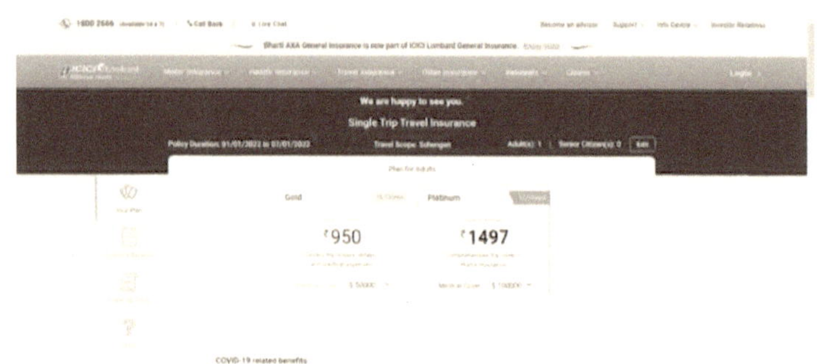

Picture64: ICICI Lombard website5[23]

7. And one can proceed to buy. I did not attempt any further as I would need to provide many more details.

---

[22] *Supra note 19 at 94*
[23] *Supra note 19 at 94*

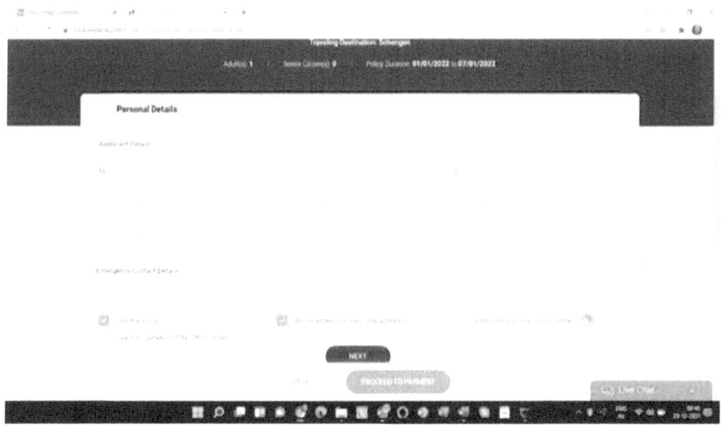

Picture65: ICICI Lombard website6[24]

8. While filling in these details, there is a question about pre-existing disease (now or in the past) and only four options exist:

a. Liver disease
b. Kidney disease
c. Heart disease
d. Cancer

So, I am not sure whether a person like me will be able to answer this correctly. I selected cancer and got the following response:

[24] *Ibid*

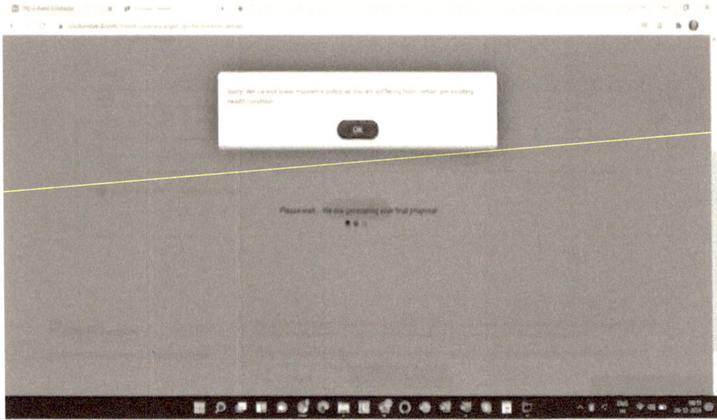

Picture66: ICICI Lombard website7[25]

Now this could be a combination of my age also (I had filled in correctly). But, then most likely a large number of policies cannot be issued. Answered correctly, I believe a large number of travellers will have one of these four conditions.

9. It seems the premium is based on number of travel days only and the age does not matter (the quote was given before asking my age and did not change even after).

10. At the bottom of the page (mostly we will not scroll down) I could see some FAQs clearly 'any pre-existing disease declared or not declared will not be covered.'

[25] *Supra note 20 at 75*

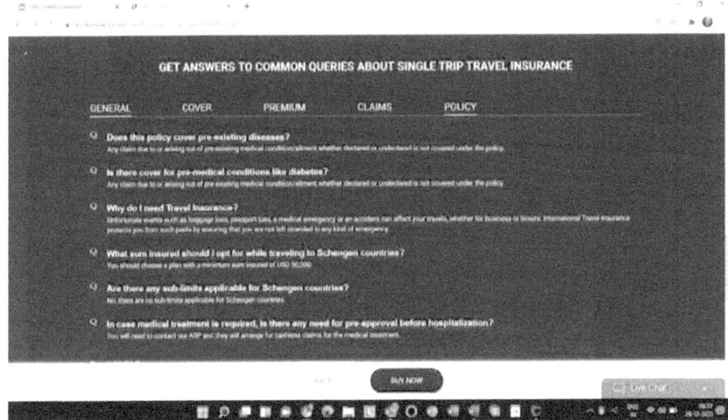

Picture67: ICICI Lombard website8[26]

So what does this SC ruling mean?

11. Attempted the same with TATA AIG it asked Date of Birth as first question. It says 'I agree to terms and condition' but does not force to read. Easier than ICICI Lombard, I felt, but there were no FAQs to say anything about the pre-existing disease. The terms did say 'pre-existing disease excluded.'

[26] *Supra note 20 at 75*

Terms And Conditions

General Exclusions

4. serving in any branch of the Military or Armed Forces of any country, whether in peace or War, and in such an event We, upon written notification by You, shall return the pro rata premium for any such period of service during the Trip; or

8. any loss arising out of War, civil war, invasion, insurrection, revolution, act of foreign enemy

Picture68: TATA AIG website1[27]

I remember having purchased travel insurance policy many times online, on the eve of travel, never looked into conditions and never realized this question about 'pre-existing' conditions (or I lied perhaps cannot recollect I do have high bp and cholesterol and are controlled through medication. Would this fall under any of the four diseases mentioned above by ICICI Lombard? I am not sure. So, who is at fault? Customer will suffer for sure.

I have another case (non-travel insurance) where my brother went through CABG (heart bypass surgery) the insurance company (CARE Health Insurance Company) kept giving approvals, he went through the surgery and on the day of discharge, at midnight, refused to honour saying he had a pre-existing condition which was not disclosed. We had to pay 4.5lacs on the spot to come home from the hospital. We have not received the claim from the company despite over 6

[27] *TATA AIG | Buy Car, Bike, Health & Travel Insurance Online*

months' chase. So, my recommendation is to be careful in the beginning itself, I would recommend avoid buying this online or through agents who fill in the forms on your behalf and you do not even realize what has been mentioned on the form.

These cases bring out that the Organisations in question are not resilient as these are not customer caring Organisations.

35. Operational Resilience Policy (Bank of England) vs Operational Resilience Guidance (Central Bank of Ireland)

First the actual names of the documents

a) Bank of England (BoE) has multiple documents (and hence complicated and complex). One of them is Statement of Policy Organisational resilience, March 2021.

b) Central Bank of Ireland (CBI) has just one document Cross Industry Guidance on Operational Resilience, December 2021.

I went through both, and my initial impression is that Central Bank of Ireland has kept it easy, simple to read, understand, and implement.

Some reasons that I believe so:

1. It has defined Operational Resilience.
2. Also defines difference between Operational Risk and Operational Resilience.
3. Value of Operational Risk has been defined (so 'what's in it for me' is clear).
4. Core Principles have been defined.
5. Three Pillars of Operational Resilience make a lot of sense.
6. Clearly states that the Board is responsible for Operational Resilience.
7. There are actually guidelines (15 of them) rarely seen such a guideline/ guidance document.
8. Does mention BIA, RTO, RPO, MAO etc. hence is more meaningful.
9. Clearly specifies what is to be done in a test.
10. Talks of Continual Improvement specifically.

Some similarities are:

1. Both focus on overall impact on community/ society/ financial system (market).
2. Both talk of recovery of A good point is that both (BoE and CBI) talk of recovery of the basic minimum (critical/ important business services). And the recovery is expected at service level (not process level as most of us would have done in the past).
3. Both greatly talk of supply chain continuity.
4. Both are non-prescriptive (which means flexibility for Organisations while implementing and is good).

(in both cases, the penalties/ implications of non-compliance are not known to me yet).

I go up to an extent to say that Operational Resilience is to be achieved through BCM, and should then lead to Organisational Resilience, which is much more than BCM, Risk, Crisis, Information/ Cyber security etc. put together (see infographic). Organisational Resilience is the need of the hour for all Organisations. I define a Resilient Organisation as one that is 'Risk Managing, Learning, and Continually Improving.'

36 Million Dollars Answer-2

Sales & Marketing Misalignment Can Cost Businesses $1 trillion per year!

(Based on an HBR article "Are Your Marketing and Sales Teams on the Same Page Kelsey Raymond")

1. 90% of sales & marketing professionals reported misalignment in terms of strategy, process, culture, and content
2. All of them said that this harmed business and customers
3. 97% said the marketing crated content without involving sales
4. They also said that the content pushed the 'product' rather than 'value' or 'solving problems'

This sales-marketing misalignment is estimated to cost businesses more than USD1 trillion per year!

The article suggests some benefits of aligning both departments:

1. Increased speed of change
2. Creative problem solving
3. Employee retention

If misalignment of two departments can cost this much, you can imagine what happens in the Organisation as a whole (my example of a monster truck that has twenty giant wheels -refer Picture1 that need to be kept balanced and aligned).

The article also recommends some remedies:

1. Audit the content you have to enable revenue generation
2. Have marketing team members shadow sales calls
3. Hold regular brainstorming sessions with sales and marketing team members
4. Provide the sales team with knowledge about prospects for their sales calls

The remedies are equally applicable to the remaining eighteen wheels also! This is how Organisations will become resilient.

I go up to an extent to say that Operational Resilience is to be achieved through BCM, and should then lead to Organisational Resilience, which is much more than BCM, Risk, Crisis, Information/ Cyber security etc. put together (see infographic). Organisational Resilience is the need of the hour for all Organisations. I define a Resilient Organisation as one that is 'Risk Managing, Learning, and Continually Improving.'

37 Renewals Insurance and Warranties Is It Ethical Business?

Here are two real cases.

1. *My brother purchased health insurance from company A. He then got the policy ported to company B (CARE Health), along with an add-on insurance component. He then had to undergo CABG (Heart bypass) surgery. On the night of discharge, the company refused the payment saying, 'he had an existing ailment which was not disclosed'. He had to make the payment from his own pocket but kept chasing the company (including the treating hospital, IRDA the insurance regulator in India, the ombudsman etc.) ut to no resolution. In between, the policy renewal came up. He made that payment, and the policy was renewed.*

Here is the question if the insurance company had the view that the policy holder had concealed some facts in the past due to which one claim was rejected, then why/ how did they renew the policy because that clause would be invoked with his each claim in future and all claims would be rejected this meant the company would keep charging him without providing the services this is unethical practice according to me. If there is any such customer who has hidden some facts while buying a policy, the insurance company should cancel the policy. I hope I am making the sense, and while my brother later lost battle to cancer, and is no more with us, I wish to take this case to the court on Ethical basis not chasing the old, rejected case, but how/ why did the company charge and renewed his policy when they were going to reject his claims!

2. *I purchased a Lenovo laptop in Jan 2021, with 1year onsite warranty. In December 2021, I realized that the battery backup had*

reduced to about 50%. I left a message through their website no response in 2-3 days; found an email id from their website and wrote a mail no response in 2-3 days; attempted through their bot assistant it won't be able to understand and went into loop but was finally able to put me in touch with a real support person. I spent at least 30 minutes with this person, who ran some diagnostics on my machine and said it was 30% degraded (in 11 months of use) and there was nothing wrong with it, so no further action while my expectation was that the battery should be replaced as the warranty was still on. The person refused saying that I could escalate, but he wouldn't be able to offer a replacement to me because there was nothing wrong with the battery and it was only 30% degraded. While I was about to disconnect in dissatisfaction, this person offered me 'can I offer you an extended warranty beyond the current one?' I was shocked what kind of a question it was you were not helping me within my existing warranty, but you were expecting me to buy an extended warranty what for? You would reject my claim even under that warranty!

So, once again the same question is it ethical business to offer extension of warranty when the current warranty is not assisting the customer?

Now I bring the focus on Organisational Resilience. Building, maintaining, and enhancing relationships is critical in Organisational Resilience program. In both the cases, by their act CARE and Lenovo did not take care of relationship with their interested party.

This gets linked with the complaint management process of the company. All Organisations have a common process 'Customer Complaint Management Process.' A big challenge is that most Organisations have outsourced this process. Some to exceedingly small Organisations. I will not mind naming an Organisation from India Airtel. One would feel that perhaps they have outsourced their Customer Support/ Complaint

Management Process to a corner shop! The next challenge is 'what is a complaint?'

1. A mail with 'complaint' in the subject line.
2. A dissatisfaction expressed in any manner:

a. Written
b. Spoken
c. Interpreted (face expressions, body language, changing the supplier/ service provider/ hospital)
d. Got from third party

So, I recommend that you go back to your customer complaint department / process and see what is happening in your Organisation. Specially, if you have outsourced the call centre/ complaint management be aware of what is being said to which customer. Offering extension of warranty/ renewal of policy when the existing policy/ warranty has not worked well should be crafted very well and carefully.

Truly Resilient Organisations would take all above to be complaints and will take them to closure hopefully to the satisfaction of the customer. My experience with Dharamshila Narayana Super specialty Hospital, New Delhi is that their call center will divert you to the concerned department/ person and that's it! Whether the call is resolved and to the customer's satisfaction is not in their scope and I assume that it's in on one's scope.

I go up to an extent to say that Operational Resilience is to be achieved through BCM, and should then lead to Organisational Resilience, which is much more than BCM, Risk, Crisis, Information/ Cyber security etc. put together (see the picture below). Organisational Resilience is the need of the hour for all Organisations. I define a Resilient Organisation as one that is 'Risk Managing, Learning, and Continually Improving.'

38 Guest Chapter-1!: Organizational Resilience The People Aspect

Haripriya

MBCI | Certified Operational Resilience Professional | ISO22301 LA| ISO27001 LA| ISO27701

Employees are the most important assets of any organization. Behind all the machines, automation, artificial intelligence and customers, there are people propelling the world towards resilience. The term resilience is picking up so much pace that business continuity is now expanding its wings to encompass wider aspects of organization.

Any business has its own chain of people from end user, employees, suppliers, outsourced partners, the list can go on. Business continuity has given much emphasis to ensure continuity of business processes as per agreed contractual requirements. While people supporting the critical business processes are expected to play their part when crisis strikes, not much attention is provided to check whether they are resilient enough to continue performing their role fulfilling their responsibilities as though nothing happened.

Business Continuity is the means to Operational and thereby Organizational Resilience. A truly resilient organization will have resilient people.

Disruptions and crises happen in many ways and at varied levels and hence BCM focuses on developing and validating strategies and plans to manage the consequences. But while developing the plans no one can predict the impact people involved in the business delivery and continuity may have especially emotionally and psychologically. Does mental health matter in BCM?

As per some key facts shared by WHO regarding mental health in emergencies published on 16th March 2022

- Almost all people affected by emergencies will experience psychological distress, which for most people will improve over time.
- Among people who have experienced war or other conflict in the previous 10 years, one in five (22%) will have depression, anxiety, post-traumatic stress disorder, bipolar disorder or schizophrenia.

Covid 19 pandemic has definitely had severe repercussions for societies, health system and economies. Countless families have lost their near and dear ones including livelihood. Children and young adults have missed out on socializing leaving a deep impact on their mental and emotional health. Almost all organizations have most part of their workforce in the age group of 20 to 40 that is more vulnerable to stress.

How can BCM integrate this aspect of ensuring mental and psychological well-being of their employees? It is important and imperative that the critical support staff and the backup resources are assessed for their resilience capabilities through training, exercise and personal discussions regarding their preparedness. While BCM focuses on service restoration and operational resilience focuses on customer operational impact to continue important business services, it is important that people behind these processes are given such importance, care and support.

The integrated focus on multiple areas of management leading to organizational resilience shall as part of Human Resource Management expand its coverage to understand the employees' stress levels and have employee engagement initiatives to address this concern. Involving the families of employees, especially critical support staff as part of overall BCM preparedness, providing them key insight into the recovery processes involving their family member is one way of demonstrating care and support. The families of employees are after all one of the interested parties in the BCM program.

ISO22301:2019, the latest version of the standard has included resilience in the title and ISO22330 provides guidelines for people aspects of business continuity and the possible strategies for improving these aspects as part of overall response.

Nevertheless, a good leadership that demonstrates care for their people and building a resilient work force that can withstand the crisis and support response and recovery is the key for organizational resilience.

39 Guest Chapter-2!: Business Continuity Management- Practices and Worth

Ashish Kumawat

Ashish Kumawat is a security professional who has worked with Reliance Group Support Services (a subsidiary of Reliance Industries Ltd.) for over 8 years.

Presently, he is pursuing PhD in Public Policy and Law from Central University of Rajasthan.

Business Continuity Management (BCM) is a crucial and all-encompassing organizational process that aims to proactively identify, mitigate, and address potential risks, threats, and vulnerabilities that could disrupt essential business operations. This comprehensive strategy involves establishing safeguards and measures to ensure seamless continuity before, during, and after disruptive events such as pandemics, natural disasters, cyberattacks, economic downturns, and supply chain disruptions. The goal of BCM is to bolster an organization's resilience and minimize the adverse impacts of disruptions, facilitating a rapid and effective recovery that ensures the uninterrupted provision of vital services. This, in turn, supports maintaining the organization's reputation, meeting stakeholder expectations, satisfying customers, and safeguarding employee well-being.

Let us have a look at BCM's key components:

1. *Risk Assessment and Business Impact Analysis (BIA)*: It includes identifying potential risks, evaluating their potential impact on critical business functions, and assessing vulnerabilities. For instance, a comprehensive risk analysis might uncover cyberattacks as a significant threat. Based on the BIA, it becomes evident that a cyber event could result in substantial financial loss and reputational damage, prompting the organization to bolster cybersecurity measures and develop robust incident response plans.

2. *Business Continuity Plan (BCP):* Stemming from risk assessments and the BIA, the BCP outlines essential strategies, procedures, and contingency plans needed to maintain core operations during disruptive incidents. For example, a manufacturing company operating in an earthquake-prone region might craft a BCP incorporating redundancy measures and resilient infrastructure to ensure uninterrupted production.

3. *Crisis Management:* The establishment of a Crisis Management Team (CMT) responsible for overseeing crisis response actions is crucial. For instance, in the event of a major cyber incident, an airline would activate a CMT to swiftly manage the situation, mitigate its effects, and facilitate a rapid recovery process.

4. *Disaster Recovery Planning (DRP):* This component focuses on the restoration of systems following a disaster. For example, a cloud services provider might employ multiple geographically distributed data centers with real-time replication to ensure uninterrupted services even if one data center becomes compromised.

5. *Testing and Training:* It is integral to validating the efficiency of BCM plans and ensuring that staff are familiar with their roles during crises. To illustrate, a retail chain might simulate supply chain interruptions to pinpoint process weaknesses, refine response protocols, and enhance staff preparedness.

6. *Continuous Improvement:* BCM is an ongoing process that necessitates constant assessment, adaptation, and learning from past experiences. An online retailer's response to a ransomware attack exemplifies this, as it utilized post-incident analysis to strengthen cybersecurity measures and enhance incident response protocols.

The successful implementation of BCM is rooted in real-world application and insights derived from actual incidents[28]. To fully integrate BCM, it is imperative to consider interested parties and their respective roles. ISO 22313:2020[29] recognizes the critical role of "interested parties" in the effective execution of a Business Continuity Management System (BCMS). These parties are individuals or groups significantly impacted by or

---

[28] *Contingency and business continuity planning best practices | SAP Insights. (n.d.). SAP. https://www.sap.com/insights/contingency-continuity-planning-best-practices.html*

[29] *ISO 22313:2020. (n.d.). ISO. https://www.iso.org/standard/75107.html*

influencing the organization's continuity efforts, underscoring the need for a comprehensive and strategic approach to business continuity.

Engaging various stakeholders is pivotal in ensuring the efficacy of Business Continuity Management. These interested parties play pivotal roles in shaping an organization's capacity to endure disruptions, sustain operations, and protect its reputation. Key interested parties and their roles include employees, clients, vendors and partners, investors and shareholders, regulatory authorities, government agencies, and the media/public.

Implementing successful BCM through stakeholder engagement requires consistent communication, collaboration, and consultation throughout the BCM process. BCM relies on a robust communication strategy encompassing regular updates and interaction with relevant stakeholders. Risk assessments help identify potential impacts on interested parties, facilitating adaptations to business continuity strategies.

The concept of interested parties aligns with broader stakeholder management principles, fostering stronger relationships and enhancing organizational resilience. Effective BCM implementation necessitates commitment from management and leadership to seamlessly embed BCM into organizational practices.

The foundation of BCM is closely intertwined with ISO 31000[30], which offers a structured framework for risk

[30] *ISO 31000:2018.* (2022, February 4). ISO. https://www.iso.org/standard/65694.html

management, enhancing an organization's ability to manage uncertainties effectively. It emphasizes principles such as integrated and tailored risk management, inclusivity, transparency, timeliness, balance, and continuous improvement. The ISO 31000 framework encompasses key steps, including context establishment, risk identification, analysis, evaluation, treatment, monitoring, review, communication, and consultation. By adhering to these principles and steps, organizations can establish robust risk management practices aligned with BCM objectives.

Business Continuity Management offers *a multitude of benefits* that significantly contribute to an organization's success:

1. *Enhanced Reputation and Consumer Confidence*: Effective BCM builds trust and reliability, bolstering an organization's reputation and customer confidence. For example, during severe weather, a swift and transparent crisis response by an airline fosters customer loyalty and engagement.

2. *Reduced Downtime and Losses*: BCM minimizes downtime and financial losses during disruptions. For illustration, a well-executed disaster recovery plan enables online businesses to swiftly transit operations to backup centers, thereby reducing revenue loss.

3. *Optimized Resource Allocation*: BCM ensures focused resource allocation to critical areas, facilitating efficient resource deployment. Allocating resources to safeguard crucial production processes, for instance, supports uninterrupted output.

4. *Competitive Edge*: Robust BCM capabilities offer a competitive edge. Demonstrating resilience attracts clients and partners seeking reliability.

5. *Regulatory Compliance*: BCM helps organizations meet regulatory standards, avoiding fines and penalties. Compliance efforts guided by BCM earn regulatory approval and positive evaluations.

6. *Employee Morale and Stakeholder Confidence:* BCM enhances employee morale by providing stability during crises. Active BCM also instils investor and partner confidence.

7. *Streamlined Recovery:* BCM ensures well-defined recovery strategies, enabling swift resumption of business activities. For example, the fire-related recovery of a retail chain, supported by alternate distribution centers, exemplifies effective BCM execution.

Overall, BCM benefits encompass minimized downtime, enhanced reputation, regulatory compliance, optimized resource allocation, and stronger stakeholder relationships. The COVID-19 pandemic of 2020 served as a global wake-up call, emphasizing the indispensable role of Business Continuity Management (BCM) in sustaining organizations amidst unprecedented disruptions. The COVID-19 pandemic underscored the importance of Business Continuity Management (BCM) through various lessons. Essential industries ensured uninterrupted operation, remote work became crucial with BCM addressing challenges, supply chain disruptions were mitigated with alternative strategies, comprehensive contingency planning aided in adapting to uncertainty, employee well-being was prioritized, crisis communication was emphasized, and digital transformation was accelerated. These lessons prompted global organizations to reevaluate BCM strategies, focusing on development, risk management, and stakeholder welfare.

Despite all benefits, implementing BCM is not devoid of challenges. These challenges can encompass complexity in identifying risks for intricate infrastructures, resource limitations for creating and maintaining comprehensive BCM programs, and obtaining senior management support. Additionally, coordinating realistic testing across large organizations, overcoming employee resistance to cultural changes, and adapting to evolving technologies and threats pose obstacles. In the Indian context, challenges[31] include vulnerability to natural disasters, insufficient infrastructure, diverse cultural/regional variations, cybersecurity risks, and regulatory compliance[32]. To surmount these challenges, Indian organizations should conduct thorough risk assessments, tailor BCM plans, invest in infrastructure and cybersecurity, and cultivate resilience through collaboration among enterprises, trade groups, and government agencies.

---

[31] *World Economic Forum. (2023). Global Risks Report. In https://www3.weforum.org/docs/WEF_Global_Risks_Report_2023.pdf. Retrieved July 20, 2023, from https://www.weforum.org/reports/global-risks-report-2023*

[32] *Regulatory quality by country, around the world | TheGlobalEconomy.com. (n.d.). TheGlobalEconomy.com. https://www.theglobaleconomy.com/rankings/wb_regulatory_quality/*

Undoubtedly, COVID-19 emphasized the pivotal role of BCM in organizational resilience. While challenges abound, businesses worldwide, including those in India, can proactively address them, adapt to changing circumstances, and foster a culture of preparedness. Effective BCM offers numerous benefits and contributes to an organization's long-term success in the face of uncertainties and disruptions.

Hypothetical Case Study: XYZ Port's BCM Plan on India's West Coast

XYZ Port is a major seaport located on the west coast of India. It manages a sizeable amount of India's marine trade, dealing with a variety of goods and serving as an important import and export gateway. The Business Continuity Management (BCM) strategy strives to protect the port's operations, reputation, and stakeholder interests by ensuring the continuity of crucial port activities during and after disruptive events.

1. Risk Assessment and Business Impact Analysis:

Risk Assessment: The risk assessment process identifies potential threats and vulnerabilities that could disrupt port operations. The key risks identified for XYZ Port include the following:

A. Natural Disasters:

- Probability: Moderate to High
- Impact: High
- Important factor for consideration: Over the past years, the west coast of India has experienced severe cyclones and severe weather events leading to temporary port closures and disruptions. It is worthwhile to highlight that as

per Global Climate Risk Index, 2021 by Germanwatch[33], India remained 7th most affected country in the world in terms of extreme weather events and associated losses in 2019

B. Cybersecurity Incidents:

- Probability: High
- Impact: Moderate to High
- Important factor for consideration: India has repeatedly seen Cyber Security Incidents and Ports are no exception to this.

C. Labour Unrest and Industrial Disputes:

- Probability: Low to Moderate
- Impact: Moderate
- Important factor for consideration: Ports are not immune from labour strikes, resulting in partial or complete port shutdowns during such incidents.

D. Supply Chain Disruptions:

- Probability: Moderate
- Impact: High
- Important factor for consideration: The port relies on several international ports for cargo handling and vessel scheduling. Supply Chain Disruptions, like strike or congestions can severely affect port operations.

---

[33] *Germanwatch. (2021). Global Climate Risk Index, 2021. In https://www.germanwatch.org/. Germanwatch e.V. Retrieved August 4, 2023, from https://www.germanwatch.org/sites/default/files/Global%20Climate%20Risk%20Index%202021_2.pdf*

Business Impact Assessment: BIA assesses potential disruptions' financial and operational impact on critical port functions. Key findings include:

A. Loss of Revenue: A one-day port closure due to a natural disaster or cybersecurity incident could result in a big loss in revenue.
B. Cargo Delay Costs: Due to cargo delays, supply chain disruptions lead to an additional cost in USDs for vessel owners and importers/exporters.
C. Reputational Damage: A significant disruption lasting over some days can lead to significant reputational damage, impacting customer confidence and attracting negative media attention.

2. Business Continuity Planning:

Crisis Management Team (CMT): A dedicated CMT comprises representatives from crucial port departments, including operations, security, IT, communications, and finance. The CMT's roles and responsibilities are defined, and backup personnel are identified.

A. Emergency Response Plan: The BCP includes a well-defined emergency response plan that outlines actions and responsibilities during different types of crises. This plan includes:

- Communication Protocols: There are established clear lines of communication, such as crisis communication platforms, emergency warning systems, and a special hotline for stakeholders.

- Evacuation Procedures: Plans for evacuating port employees, guests, and stakeholders have been created and are frequently practiced.
- Coordination with Authorities: To provide a coordinated response during major emergencies, the port works with regional authorities, emergency services, and governmental organizations.
- Redundancy and Contingency Plans: The port implements redundancy for critical systems, infrastructure, and resources to minimize downtime during disruptions. Contingency plans are developed to address alternative cargo handling and vessel scheduling during terminal closures.

B. Backup Power and Data Recovery: The BCP ensures the availability of backup power sources, such as generators and UPS systems, to support essential operations during power outages. Robust data recovery measures, including regular backups and offsite storage, protect critical port data in case of a cyber incident.

C. Open Communication and Management of Stakeholders: To keep stakeholders, such as port users, shipping lines, customs, and regulatory agencies, informed during emergencies, a thorough communication plan is devised. Press releases, social media, email alerts, and other communication channels all serve as regular update conduits.

3. Testing and Training:

A. Simulations: It comes in a variety of forms, such as computer simulations and tabletop models. These simulations allow the CMT and other important employees to debate and assess how they would react in various crisis scenarios. These activities aid in finding BCP gaps and enhancing team member collaboration.

B. Functional exercises: To evaluate their response capabilities, specific departments within the port conduct functional exercises. These drills include of emergency medical response training, cargo handling in limited regions, and vessel scheduling under emergency circumstances.

C. Full-Scale Mock-Drills and Exercises: To test coordination and communication during major emergencies, the port periodically conducts full-Scale Exercises with external agencies, including emergency services and government authorities. These drills represent scenarios like a powerful hurricane or a cyberattack on port infrastructure.

4. Continuous Improvement:

It ensures that system is always pro-active and does not allow any discrepancy to come in. it can happen in following ways:

1. Regular Review: To integrate lessons gained and handle new risks, the port refreshes its BCM strategy every year and following a significant incident. The BIA is updated often to account for adjustments to hazards and port operations.
2. 2. Industry Collaborations: The port works with other ports and trade groups to exchange best practices, keep abreast of changing threats, and develop BCM strategies. The BCM program at XYZ Port incorporates the lessons learnt from prior port accidents.

The detailed Business Continuity Management plan for XYZ Port on the west coast of India ensures that the port is resilient and capable of maintaining critical operations during disruptive events. The plan's implementation, backed by data-driven risk assessments and continuous testing, makes the port well-prepared to handle various challenges, protect stakeholder interests, and contribute to India's continued growth in maritime trade.

Adopting Business Continuity practices at XYZ Port has made its operations resilient and effective in handling various crises. The following conceived examples illustrate how BCM helped the port remain operational during challenging situations:

1. *Cyclone Resilience:* The port activated its BCP during a strong cyclone, and the CMT quickly coordinated emergency actions. To protect the welfare of the crew and the cargo, terminal operations were put on hold. However, the port's backup measures enabled a speedy return to business once the hurricane passed. Critical operations, including communication with boats and cargo tracking, were assured to be uninterrupted by redundant systems and backup power sources.
2. *Cyber Security Incident Response:* The port's IT systems were the subject of a cyberattack that disrupted communication and cargo tracking networks. The effect was reduced by the port's data recovery procedures, and business was rapidly restored. To guarantee transparency and avoid delays in vessel itineraries, the CMT efficiently interacted with port users and regulatory agencies.
3. *Labour Strike Management:* The port launched its emergency response strategy during a labor dispute that had an impact on cargo operations. To lessen the effects, the CMT collaborated with law enforcement organizations, labor unions, and port users. At other terminals, different cargo handling procedures were put in place to guarantee that vital goods got there without suffering substantial delays.

Conclusion:

Ultimately, contemporary corporate operations hinge on effective BCM, enhancing resilience through risk assessment, crisis preparedness, and ongoing improvement. Investment in BCM empowers organizations to maintain competitiveness, safeguard stakeholder interests, and ensure continuity in the face of unexpected challenges. The concept of "keeping enemies close," derived from Kautilya's "Arthashastra," underscores the strategic value of understanding, assessing, and mitigating risks. Here, the possible risks are synonymous to enemies, and they need to be studied well. Collaborative efforts, like alliances with industry peers, can bolster collective resilience. Herbert Simon's[34] insights emphasize the vital role of training in effective decision-making and problem-solving within organizations. In the realm of BCM, continuous training and involvement of personnel are key to success. Overall, a comprehensive and continuous BCM approach is essential to fully harness its benefits.

[34] *Simon, H. A. (1947). Administrative Behavior: A Study of Decision-Making Processes in Administrative Organizations.*

40 Guest Chapter-3!: "Busyness" Impact Analysis (BIA)?

Jonathan Nangor

Business Continuity & Operational Risk Manager
CBCI - Board Member, Chapter North & West Africa
Certified Operational Resilience Professional,
Lead Implementer ISO/IEC 27001:2013
Lead Implementer ISO 22301:2019
Crisis Management Professional (BS11200:2014)
ITIL 4
Certified Organizational Resilience Specialist & Implementer
Certified International Trainer and Coach

First and foremost, I would like to express my gratitude to one of the most prolific, passionate, and resilient thought leaders of the Business Continuity & Resilience industry, Daman Dev Sood. Thanks, Daman, for inspiring me!

As I decided to accept the challenge and opportunity of writing one chapter of this book, I thought it would be interesting to share with you a few things I have been reflecting on for the past weeks regarding the Business Impact Analysis (BIA) exercise.

As a BCM professional and practitioner, I believe the Business Impact Analysis (BIA) represents and remains the foundation of any strong and efficient Business Continuity Management System (BCMS).

Recently, while I was conducting BIA workshops, I realized something I had never thought about before…

What if the Business Impact Analysis was a real eye-opener that gives us the opportunity to approach a new type of BIA: the "Busyness" Impact Analysis? Why not confront the "Business" with the "Busyness" and ensure that the organization is still focused on its very purpose and core objectives? What if "Busyness" Impact Analysis was the best approach to understanding and reshaping what I would call "Organizational Busyness"? I think I should find some time (with Daman's help) to go a bit further and dig into this new concept…

In fact, discussing the description, outcome, dependencies, and criticality of each process and activity of any organization, many of those "not so obvious" but "difficult" questions suggested some reflection and analysis. The following lines are an invitation to every leader and manager who values Resilience and / or Business Continuity and who is willing to take another step toward organizational resilience.

Below are the thought-provoking questions that are meant to pave the way to make the traditional BIA a more strategic tool in today's corporate world:

- How should I consider and handle the processes that are not really impactful (or key) to the survival of my organization?

- Is there any room to improve or revamp the way those "secondary" processes are handled and managed throughout the organization?

- What is the added value of those processes for which the organization can afford a disruption over some period of time without any significant harm to the Business?

- Do the results of the Business Impact Analysis reflect the organization vision, mission, values? If not, why? What can we do for this?

- Is the organization really "Busy" on the "Business"?

- What is my organization busy at? What is the impact of that "busyness" on the processes and activities that really matter?

- Are the prioritized, essential, or critical processes (depending on how you name it in your organization) really core to the organization? To the Top Management? If yes, how do you know?

- Is the organization "taking care" of the prioritized processes related resources (including manpower) as part of the "business as usual" mode or being concerned only during the crisis mode activation?

- Should the recovery personnel be aware of the criticality of their processes only during Business Continuity Plan activation or as part of the day-to-day routine?

Since we are to spend some time in this Resilience journey (just check the news or look around you and you will agree), let us enjoy the trip and embrace every perspective, idea, thought that can help us push forward our own Resilience and serve our organizations the best way we can.

I personally think that this is the right time for every organization to become intentional in building a Culture of "Busyness disruption" in order to strengthen the Business itself and enhance the Business Continuity and Resilience capability.

41 Guest Chapter-4!: My Resilience Mantra

Dr. Shiv Dhawan

MY RESILIENCE MANTRA

I will not give in to sadness.

I will not let my thoughts control the way I feel.

I will never , ever give up.

I will stay positive and work on a solution.

My life is great with all the positive and negative things in it.

I allow myself to be happy no matter what.

I am enough and I am complete.

Reader's views on various chapters

Daman Dev Sood

Director DBD Training & Consultancy (OPC) Private Limited

International Resilience Trainer & Consultant

FBCI, FBCS, CBCI, SMIEEE, MAIMA, M.IOD, ISO 22301 LA & Expert

Certified in Cybersecurity (ISC2)

IEEE Ambassador

Past Chair IEEE Computer Society Delhi Section Chapter

Chair PR&P Standing Committee, IEEE Delhi Section

Member Champion IEEE India MOVE Partner Relations Committee

IEEE Computer Society Distinguished Contributor (Inaugural Class)

Toastmaster

Reskube Partner

Global Release - Global Emotional Impact Assessment Report click here to download complimentary copy

Video profile: https://youtu.be/TuPmBmYDIms

Email: daman@damandevsood.com

Phone: +91 9958091880 (whatsapp)

Author of "Resilience Through The Eyes of My Readers" available at notionpress.com, amazon.in, amazon.com, flipkart.com

Author of "My Experiments with Organisational Resilience: Part-I" available at notionpress.com, amazon.in, flipkart.com

Author of "COPYRIGHT Cases Resolved" available at notionpress.com, amazon.in, flipkart.com

Author of "My Experiments With BCM" available at notionpress.com, amazon.in, amazon.co.uk, amazon.com, flipkart.com, kriso.it, wob.com, barnesandnoble.com, ebook.de, books.google.co.in, fnac.com, bookdepository.com , shop.wordbookstores.com, fnac.pt, kizzybooksandmore.com

Author of the "Step by Step guide to the NCEMA 7000: Implement BCM the UAE way" - Available online at the Kindle store

CPD
MEMBER
The CPD Certification Service
DRI International
BCI Global Awards 2021 WINNER
2021 WINNER
RESKUBE
CC
bci Middle East Awards WINNER 2020
bci Fellow
FELLOW
bcs
CERTIFICATE OF RECOGNITION

My Courses

S. No.	Course	Duration	Standard/ Area	Type
1	Certified Resiliency Testing Specialist **(CPD Certified)**	3 days	Resiliency	Instructor Led Online/ Classroom
2	Certified Organisational Resilience Professional	1 day	ISO 22316:2017	Instructor Led Online/ Classroom
3	Certified Organisational Resilience Specialist	3 days	ISO 22316:2017	Instructor Led Online/ Classroom
4	Certified Risk Management Professional	1 day	ISO 31000:2018	Instructor Led Online/ Classroom
5	Certified Risk Management Specialist	3 days	ISO 31000:2018	Instructor Led Online/ Classroom
6	Practical BIA (Specialist level)	2 days	BCM	Instructor Led Online/ Classroom

S. No.	Course	Duration	Standard/ Area	Type
7	Operational Resilience Foundation	½ day	Operational Resilience	Instructor Led Online/ Classroom
8	Certified Operational Resilience Professional	1 day	Operational Resilience	Instructor Led Online/ Classroom
9	Design, Develop, and Deliver an Effective BCM Test	2 days	BCM	Instructor Led Online/ Classroom
10	Daman's Thermometer	1 day	Crisis Communication	Instructor Led Online/ Classroom
11	Possibility Thinking	1 day	Softskills	Instructor Led Online/ Classroom

S. No.	Course	Duration	Standard/ Area	Type
12	Team Work & Art of Handling Questions	1 day	Softskills	Instructor Led Online/ Classroom
13	Resiliency Testing (for top management)	2 days	Resiliency	Instructor Led Online/ Classroom
14	Cyber Resiliency Testing (for top management)	1 day	Resiliency	Instructor Led Online/ Classroom
15	Certified Delivering Excellence Specialist **(CPD Certified)**	3 days	Resiliency	Instructor Led Online/ Classroom
16	Circular Economy, Life Cycle Analysis, ESG, and Sustainable Supply Chain	1 day	Sustainability	Instructor Led Online/ Classroom

Copyrights Status

Course	Copyright Status
Organisational Resilience Specialist	Achieved
Organisational Resilience Professional	Achieved
Risk Management Professional	Achieved
Daman's thermometer	Achieved
Possibility Thinking	Achieved
Design, Develop, and Deliver an Effective BCM Test	Achieved
Practical BIA Course	Achieved
Teamwork and Art of Handling Questions	Achieved
Risk Management Specialist	Achieved
Operational Resilience Professional	Achieved
Resiliency Testing Specialist	Achieved
Delivering Excellence Specialist	Applied for

CERTIFICATE

OF

MEMBERSHIP

The CPD Certification Service
certifies that

Daman Dev Sood

is a MEMBER of
The CPD Certification Service

Providing recognised independent CPD accreditation compatible with global CPD principles.

Membership Number

17743

An initiative to increase standards of CPD provision to professionals in relevant market sectors

Date of Commencement: **9th June 2023**

Authorised Signature: G. Savage

Managing Director, The CPD Certification Service

The Coach House, Ealing Green, London W5 5ER
Email: info@cpduk.co.uk Web: www.cpduk.co.uk
Tel: 020 8840 4383

CPD
MEMBER
The CPD Certification
Service

The content of the following has been certified by The CPD Certification Service as conforming to Continuing Professional Development principles

Certified Delivering Excellence Specialist Course Training Course

MEMBER

DAMAN DEV SOOD
(017743)

Date:
July 2023

Certificate No:
47943

The Coach House, Ealing Green, London W5 5ER
E-mail: info@cpduk.co.uk Web: www.cpduk.co.uk
Tel: 020 8840 4383

The content of the following has been certified by the CPD Certification Service as conforming to continuing professional development principles

Daman's 3 Days Certified Resiliency Testing Specialist Course
Training Course

UDBHATA TECHNOLOGIES
(017491)

Date:	*Certificate No:*
May 2023	47004

The CPD Certification Service, The Coach House, Ealing Green, London W5 5ER Tel: 020 8840 4383
E-mail: info@cpduk.co.uk Web: www.cpduk.co.uk

All Pictures

Other Books

BUSINESS CONTINUITY
Implement BCM the UAE Way!
1st EDITION
STEP-BY-STEP GUIDE
AE/SCNS/NCEMA 7000:2015
TOWARDS NATIONAL RESILIENCE
Authors
DHIRAJ LAL
DAMAN DEV SOOD

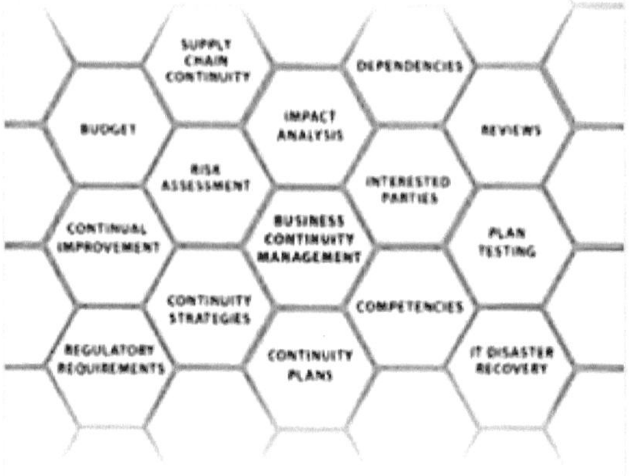
MY
EXPERIMENTS WITH
TRUTH BCM
MY BCM JOURNEY • YOUR BCM MENTOR/COMPANION
SUPPLY CHAIN CONTINUITY
DEPENDENCIES
BUDGET
IMPACT ANALYSIS
REVIEWS
RISK ASSESSMENT
INTERESTED PARTIES
CONTINUAL IMPROVEMENT
BUSINESS CONTINUITY MANAGEMENT
PLAN TESTING
CONTINUITY STRATEGIES
COMPETENCIES
REGULATORY REQUIREMENTS
CONTINUITY PLANS
IT DISASTER RECOVERY
DAMAN DEV SOOD

COPYRIGHT
Cases
Resolved

ANCHITA SOOD

DAMAN DEV SOOD

cover designed by Tanuj Sood

My EXPERIMENTS with ~~TRUTH~~ ORGANISATIONAL RESILIENCE

Part-1

DAMAN DEV SOOD

www.ingramcontent.com/pod-product-compliance
Lightning Source LLC
LaVergne TN
LVHW091325150826
845673LV00006B/1768

* 9 7 9 8 8 9 1 3 3 2 8 3 6 *